Saguaro cactus, Organ Pipe Cactus National Monument

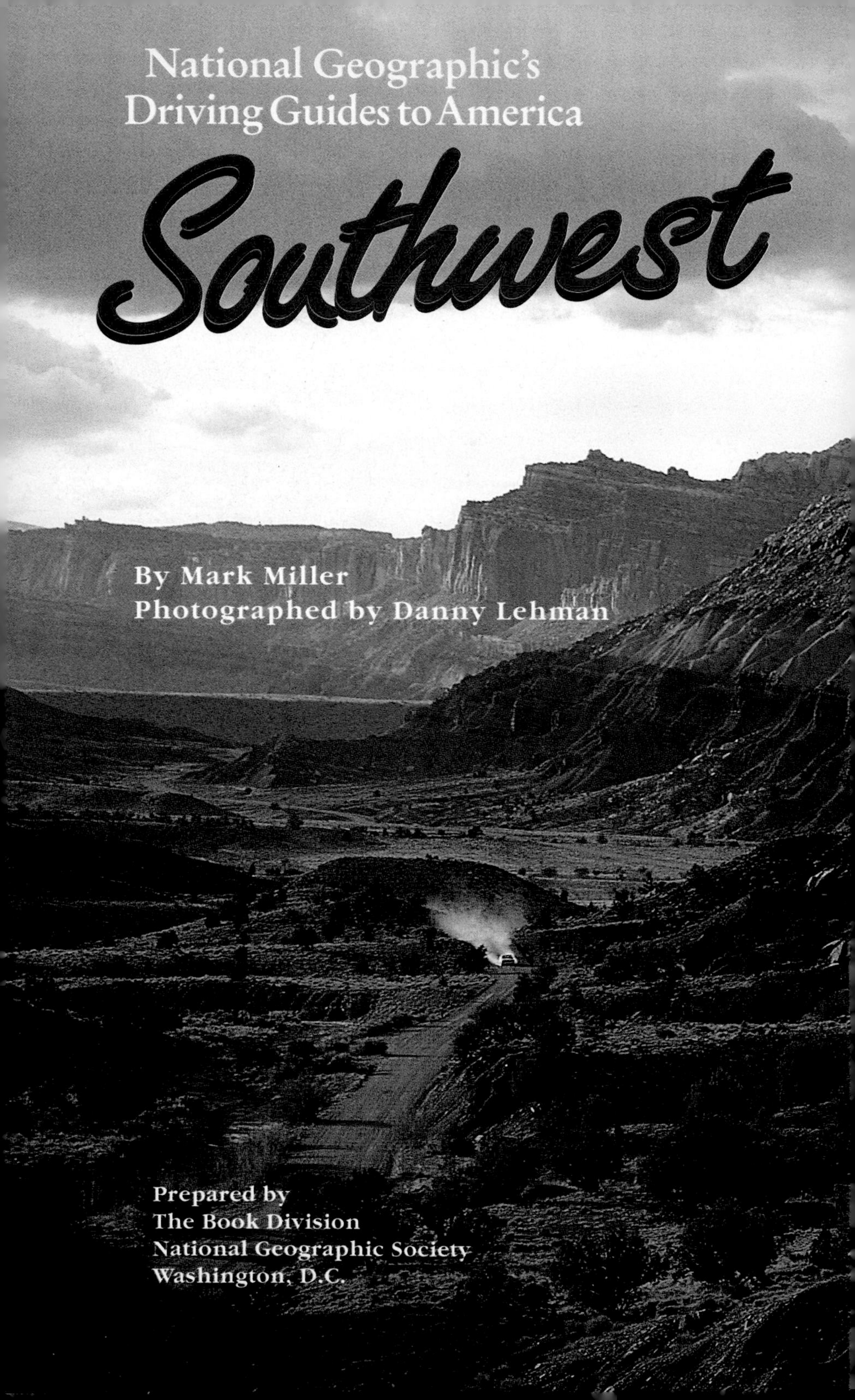

National Geographic's Driving Guides to America

Southwest

By Mark Miller
Photographed by Danny Lehman

Prepared by
The Book Division
National Geographic Society
Washington, D.C.

National Geographic's Driving Guides To America Southwest

By Mark Miller
Photographed by Danny Lehman

Published by
The National Geographic Society

Reg Murphy
President and Chief Executive Officer
Gilbert M. Grosvenor
Chairman of the Board
Nina D. Hoffman
Senior Vice President

Prepared by The Book Division

William R. Gray
Vice President and Director
Charles Kogod
Assistant Director
Barbara A. Payne
Editorial Director

4

Driving Guides to America

Elizabeth L. Newhouse
*Director of Travel Books
and Series Editor*
Cinda Rose
Art Director
Thomas B. Powell III
Illustrations Editor
Caroline Hickey, Barbara A. Noe
Senior Researchers
Carl Mehler
Map Editor and Designer

Staff for this book

Caroline Hickey
Project Manager
Mary Luders
Editor
Joan A. Wolbier
Designer

Thomas B. Powell III
Illustrations Editor
Carl Mehler
Map Editor and Designer

Sean M. Groom
Michael H. Higgins
Jennifer Emmett
Researchers

Carol Bittig Lutyk
Contributing Editor

Joseph F. Ochlak
Chief Map Researcher
Michelle H. Picard and
Mapping Specialists, Limited
Map Production
Tibor G. Tóth
Map Relief

Meredith C. Wilcox
Illustrations Assistant

Richard S. Wain
Production Project Manager
Lewis R. Bassford, Lyle Rosbotham
Production

Kevin G. Craig, Dale M. Herring,
Peggy Purdy
Staff Assistants

Diane Coleman
Indexer

Thomas B. Blabey, Nancy A. Donnelly,
Banafsheh Ghassemi
Contributors

Manufacturing and Quality Management

George V. White, *Director*
John T. Dunn, *Associate Director*
Vincent P. Ryan, *Manager*

Cover: North Window, Arches National Park, Utah

Previous pages: Capitol Reef National Park, Utah

Facing page: Montezuma Castle National Monument, Arizona

Library of Congress CIP data: page 160

Southwestern fare, San Ildefonso Pueblo, New Mexico

IDAHO

84 15 89

Ogden-
Bear Lake
Ogden 16

80 191

Great
Salt
Lake

84 WYOMING FLAMING
GORGE N.R.A.

Salt Lake
City 150

80 191 DINOSAUR
NAT. MON.

Salt Lake
Area ★★

Green River-
Flaming Gorge ★

Utah
Lake

Provo 40 40 40 COLO.

36 6 191 139

89

U T A H

6 Green
50 River

6 50

15 50 70 70

NEVADA

70 24 24 ARCHES N.P.

Bryce and
Capitol Reef ★★ 24 95 GLEN CANYONLANDS
NAT. PARK

130 BRYCE
CANYON
N.P. CAPITOL
REEF
N.P. CANYON Arches ★★
and Canyons

Cedar City 143 12 191

ZION
N.P. NATIONAL

15 Zion-North Rim
Loop ★★ 276

St. George RECREATION AREA

89

Kayenta 160 64 64

67 Tuba
City 160 Bloomfield

GRAND Navajo-Hopi 264 666 44 CHACO
CANYON Drive CULTURE
N.H.P.

LAKE MEAD
N.R.A. GRAND
CANYON
N.P. CANYON DE
CHELLY N.M. Historical
New Mexico ★

93 180 89 191 Gallup

Grand Canyon
and South ★ 40 PETRIFIED
FOREST
N.P. 602 40

40 89 Flagstaff 180 40 61 53

Phoenix Northwest
Loop 93 Prescott A R I Z O N A Mogollon
Plateau 180 EL MALPAIS
N.M. Middle
Pueblos

The
Coast 89 17 260 Concho 36 60

CALIFORNIA 95 60 87 Springerville

10 60 60 Salt River
Basin ★ Rocks
and
Ghosts ★

95 Phoenix 77 Globe 191 180

85 10 60 70

8 8 79 77 70

Yuma ★ Tucson-
Organ Pipe Loop 10

ORGAN PIPE
CACTUS
N.M. 86 SAGUARO
N.P. Tucson SAGUARO
N.P. 10

85 19 The ★★
Border Region

U.S. 82 191
MEXICO Nogales U.S.
MEXICO

Contents

7

Pipe Spring National Monument, Utah

Desert Traveling

Touring the Southwest, especially in summer, requires heightened attention to personal well-being, particularly if you're headed for desert country. Water is of paramount importance. Wide-open spaces can mean few motorist services. Even if your vehicle is air-conditioned, heat and low humidity can rapidly dehydrate you. Stow a gallon of water in your trunk for emergencies, and keep another close at hand. Make a point of drinking more than usual. Absolutely essential: a hat or cap, sunscreen, and sturdy walking shoes with good traction. Take sunglasses—squinting won't help you see through desert glare, which can quickly lead to eye fatigue. Don't forget to take your binoculars and, most important, a pen and postage stamps for sending postcards.

8

*W*hile writing this book, I sometimes felt like a parent preparing to send a son or daughter off to college—knowing that no matter how much advice I can offer, in the end (and happily so) your adventure will be a uniquely personal voyage of discovery. That's especially true of the Southwest, where landscapes and life zones, climates and cultures, and histories and heritages are as diverse as the points on a compass rose.

But there are some things I can promise: In ancient cliff dwellings and pueblo ruins, centuries-old mission churches, Spanish colonial villages, Old West towns, and Indian communities, you'll find a sense of the past such as you may have never experienced. And astonishing landscapes—canyons, mesas, buttes, arches, and spires whose colossal scale and vivid colors compel wonder; painted deserts that make you sigh; mountains so imposing that Indian people hold them sacred; solitude so deep the only sound will be the beating of your heart. Visit only a few sites figuring large in the Southwest's historical pageant since the arrival of Europeans in the 1500s, and you'll move closer to understanding the conflicting forces of human nature—often heroic, sometimes heartbreaking—that created the region's extraordinary character and gave it a personality able to seduce even the most casual visitor.

I can offer some practical advice too. Although the Southwest's range of elevations blurs seasonal distinctions, spring and fall weather is usually moderate, as are winter months at lower altitudes. Double check your watch in Arizona. The state is on mountain-standard time year round and thus, except on the Navajo Indian Reservation, does not observe daylight-savings time. Don't assume that a map dot with a name means a service station; in lonely regions, keep your tank topped off. Finally, the Southwest's powerful light, when overhead, can bleach the region's subtle hues—a good reason for photographing landscapes in early morning and evening.

There's an old Spanish saying that "the lands of the sun expand the soul." I can promise you that as well.

MARK MILLER

*N*ATIONAL GEOGRAPHIC'S DRIVING GUIDES TO AMERICA invite you on memorable road trips through the United States and Canada. Intended both as travel planners and companions, each volume guides you on preplanned tours over a wide variety of terrain to the best places to see and things to do. The authors, expert regional travel writers, star-rate (from none to two ★★) the drives and points of interest to make sure you don't miss their favorites.

All distances and drive times are approximate (if you linger, as you should, plan on considerably more time). Recommended seasons are the best times to go, but roads and sites are open all year unless otherwise noted. Besides the stated days of operation, many sites close on national holidays. For the most up-to-date site information, it's best to call ahead when possible.

Then, with this book and a road map, set off on your adventure through this awesomely beautiful land.

Sunset at Monument Valley, Utah

9

MAP KEY and ABBREVIATIONS

Geological Area (National)
National Conservation Area — N.C.A.
National Historical Park — N.H.P.
National Historic Site — N.H.S.
National Memorial
National Monument — NAT. MON., N.M.
National Park — N.P.
National Recreation Area — N.R.A.

National Forest — NAT. FOREST., N.F.
National Grassland,-s — N.G.

Migratory Bird Refuge
National Wildlife Refuge — N.W.R.

State Park — S.P.
Regional Park

Indian Reservation — IND.RES. I.R. INDIAN RES.

ADDITIONAL ABBREVIATIONS

Cr.	*Creek*
Mt.-s.	*Mountain-s*
NAT.	*National*
N.H.L.	*National Historic Landmark*
PKWY.	*Parkway*
PT.	*Point*
RD.	*Road*
RFC. AREA	*Recreation Area*
S.H.P.	*State Historic,-al Park*
S.H.S.	*State Historic Site*
S.M.	*State Monument*

POPULATION

● **Phoenix**	500,000 and over
● **Albuquerque**	50,000 to under 500,000
● Cedar City	under 50,000

Featured Drive

Interstate Highway — 40

U.S. Federal Highway — 89

State Road — 68

County, Local, Indian Reservation, or Mexican Federal Road — 7

National Historic Trail

Railroad

State or National Border

Boundaries
FOREST   I.R.   N.P., N.R.A.

■ Point of Interest

★ State Capital

Ι Dam

= Falls

+ Elevation, Peak

)(Pass

● **270 miles** ● **3 to 4 days** ● **Spring through late autumn** ● **Roads are good throughout.**

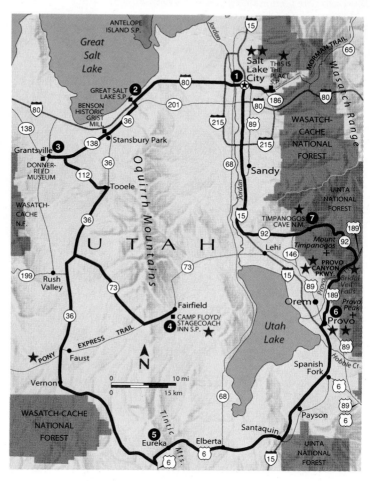

Sego, or mariposa, lily

Once forsaken, the Wasatch Range between Provo and Ogden has been transformed by Mormon settlement into one of the most prosperous, culturally vibrant urban areas in the intermountain West. Home to 80 percent of Utah's residents, this is also where 19th-century mining booms gone bust left out-of-the-way towns with histories brighter than their futures. The Great Salt Lake sweeps west into a briny haze veiling the last stretch of wild America crossed by covered wagon emigrants. This drive begins in Salt Lake City and ends in Provo and the recreational wonderland just east, where trout-fishing canyons and quiet farming valleys notch into national forests.

Marking the Mormon Trail's end and the triumph of Brigham Young's 1847 odyssey to found a "City of Zion" is sprawling ❶ **Salt Lake City**★★ *(Visitor Center 801-521-2868)*, Utah's largest city and its cultural, political, and spiritual center. Start your driving tour downtown by taking State Street to **Capitol Hill**★. The Gothic Revival **Council Hall** on your right houses the **Utah Travel Council** and the **Utah Tourism and Recreation Information Center** *(N. State and 300 North Sts. 801-538-1030)*, a treasury of free advice.

The nation's capitol was the model for the copper-domed **Utah State Capitol**★ *(N. State and 300 North Sts. 801-538-3000)*. The rotunda of Utah granite, Georgia marble, and polished brass was completed in 1915. Inside, wall and ceiling murals depict Utah history one floor above

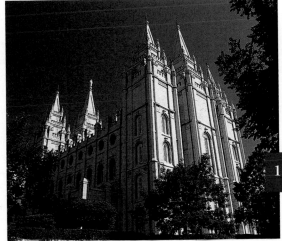

Salt Lake Temple, Salt Lake City

11

exhibits celebrating the Beehive State's 29 counties. Free brochures suggest walking tours and offer bits of history and lore about the capitol and its 38 landscaped acres.

Drive west on 300 North Street and loop through the **Marmalade District**★ (also known as the Capitol Hill Historic District), a dessert tray of Victorian homes dating from the 1850s to the 1890s. Early residents tended fruit orchards and gave their streets names like Plum, Quince, and Apricot, hence the nickname.

Continue on to the three-story, Grecian-style **Pioneer Memorial Museum**★★ *(300 N. Main St. 801-538-1050. Closed Sun. Sept.-May ; donations)*, devoted to Utah history and the Mormon saga. Don't miss the antique farm implements, carriages, and vehicles in the carriage house.

Landscaped grounds, footpaths, and courtyards inside the 10-acre walled enclave of **Temple Square**★★ *(S. Temple and Main Sts. 801-240-2534)* surround the six-towered **Salt Lake Temple**★★, best-known symbol of the Church of Jesus Christ of Latter-day Saints. Quarrymen started cutting its granite blocks in 1853, assembling base walls 9 feet thick to support the building, which rises 210 feet,

Old Deseret Village, This Is The Place State Park

12

like an explosion of light. The east tower is capped by a 12-foot-high gilded statue of the Angel Moroni, who, according to church history, delivered ancient records to Joseph Smith. (Smith founded the church in 1830.) Like all LDS temples, this one is open only to Mormons in good standing, but free guided tours of the Temple Square leave every few minutes from the center of the square.

Declared a National Civil Engineering Landmark, the **Mormon Tabernacle**★★ *(801-240-5234)* seats 6,500 beneath an 80-foot-high oval dome 150 feet wide and 250 feet long. One of the world's largest unsupported domes, it is famed for its astounding acoustics—visitors at one end can hear a pin dropped 170 feet away on the other. Sunday morning broadcasts and Thursday evening rehearsals by the world-famous Mormon Tabernacle Choir, accompanied by an 11,623-wood pipe organ producing over 140 tone colors, are open to the public. (Organ recitals are usually held daily at noon.)

Some of the Mormon faith's most sacred artifacts are cherished at the **Museum of Church History and Art**★ *(45 N. West Temple St. 801-240-3310)*. Among its treasures is the original handwritten manuscript of the Book of Mormon. Dictated to a scribe by church founder Joseph Smith, it is the fundamental scripture of the Latter-day Saints.

Salt Lake City was only seven years old when Brigham Young moved his first wife and their six children into **Beehive House** *(67 E. South Temple St. 801-240-2671)*. Filled with elegant furniture, sterling silver, and crystal, the adobe residence is named for the wood-carved beehive on the roof, a Mormon symbol of industriousness.

Trains still come and go at the **Rio Grande Depot** *(300 S. Rio Grande St. 801-364-8562)*, a temple of travel built in 1910. Its muscular flair reflects the confidence inspired by the first buckling of the steel belt across America's midsection. The high-ceilinged waiting room does double duty as the gallery of the **Utah Historical Society Museum** *(801-533-3500. Mon.-Sat.)*, where family portraits of flinty-eyed patriarchs ponder an original covered wagon and a copy of a handcart. Anyone who shipped off to war by rail will find the sense of nostalgia in the depot's **Rio Grande Café** stronger than the aroma of frying enchiladas.

In 1902 silver magnate Thomas Kearns completed a house to match his résumé: U.S. senator and owner of the *Salt Lake City Tribune*. Driving east on South Temple Street toward the University of Utah, you'll pass the politico's 28-room monument to himself, which eventually became the **Governor's Mansion** *(603 E. South Temple St. 801-538-1005. April-Dec. Tues. and Thurs.)*. It's filled with Victorian furniture and decorations as fancy as the exterior.

The 1,494-acre hillside campus of the **University of Utah★,** christened in 1850, is shaded by over 9,500 trees representing some 300 varieties. They are part of the university's **Red Butte Garden and Arboretum★** *(801-581-5322. Closed Mon. Oct.-April; adm. fee),* which also includes a 25-acre garden of shrubs and flower beds surrounded by 100 acres of natural foothills. The Art and Architecture Center holds the **University of Utah Museum of Fine Arts★★** *(1530 E. South Campus Dr. 801-581-7332),* the state's preeminent collection, especially rich in American art and furniture. Utah firearms tycoon Val Browning's collection of European art spans five centuries. Dinosaur skeletons await next door at the **Utah Museum of Natural History** *(University St. and Presidents Circle. 801-581-4303. Adm. fee),* a showcase of discoveries made in Utah's rich fossil beds. There are also an excellent survey of the state's mining history and an outstanding mineral collection.

Nearby, **Fort Douglas** preserves a variety of antique architecture, including 19th-century brick officer's housing, an adobe house, barracks, and sandstone buildings. The **Fort Douglas Military Museum** *(Bldg. 32, Potter St. 801-588-5188. Tues.-Sat.)* celebrates the all-black Buffalo Soldiers battalion, respected by Ute warriors for their battlefield gallantry. The museum stands near the parade ground, with old artillery pieces on one side.

Continue south on Wasatch Boulevard, bearing left to join Foothill Drive and then Sunnyside Avenue, which leads to **Emigration Canyon** and **This Is The Place State Park★** *(2601 Sunnyside Ave. 801-584-8391)*. Here, on July 24, 1847, Brigham Young realized he'd found the haven from persecution he promised his 148 weary pilgrims.

Famous Ancestors?

Ever wondered if you're *really* related to that famous person your grandmother insists is your kin? If the notable was born before 1900, odds are the answer lies in Salt Lake City's **Family History Library** *(35 N. West Temple St. 801-240-2331. Mon.-Sat.),* the world's most extensive genealogical archive. Why here? Mormon teachings hold that family ties continue into eternity; ancestral research is thus crucial to Mormons wishing to retroactively bring ancestors into the faith. After a short briefing at the FamilySearch Center in the **Joseph Smith Memorial Building** *(South Temple and Main Sts. 801-240-4085. Mon.-Sat.),* you can use the center's computer database to find out if it actually was your very own Uncle Eli who invented the cotton gin.

13

14

Great Salt Lake State Park

The Salt Lake Basin looked so forbidding, Young was convinced that no outsiders would covet it. According to legend, he said, "This is the right place," ending the long trek from a failed Mormon colony in Illinois.

The park's **Old Deseret Village★★** (April–mid-Oct.; adm. fee) features historical buildings moved from around the valley. In summer, Young's picket-fenced farmhouse is open for tours, and living history docents in pioneer dress demonstrate frontier skills and cooking. The park is also the site of **This Is The Place Monument,** the terminus of the **Mormon Pioneer National Historic Trail** from Nauvoo, Illinois. A 4.2-mile segment of the 1,400-mile trail is preserved as a footpath through Emigration Canyon, leaving Emigration Canyon Road at signpost 52.

As you head west from Salt Lake City on I-80, the first thing you'll see when exiting for ❷ **Great Salt Lake State Park** (801-250-1822) is the Moorish-style Saltair Pavilion. Reminiscent of turn-of-the-century spas, this swimming center is the place to wade in to find out if stories about the lake's buoyancy are true. Be forewarned though— salinity can reach up to 27 percent (about seven times that of the ocean), stinging the eyes.

Just northwest of Stansbury Park is the **Benson Historic Grist Mill** (Utah- 138. 801-882-7678. Mem. Day–Labor Day Tues.-Sat.), built in 1854 to grind flour for Mormon kitchens. The building is one of Utah's oldest, assembled without nails by using mortised beams and rawhide strips.

The worst calamity on the emigrant trail to California had its beginning near here. In 1846 the 87-member Donner-Reed party tried to save time by cutting across the **Great Salt Lake Desert,** but soon found their wagons mired in sticky salt. Late reaching the Sierra Nevada, they were stranded near the summit by early winter snows. Forty perished in a horrific ordeal of starvation that reduced some survivors to cannibalism. The tale's prologue is told at the **Donner-Reed Museum** *(Clark and Cooley Sts. 801-884-3348. By appt.)* in ❸ **Grantsville,** a map dot of adobe homes and poplar-plumed avenues founded in 1850. The archive holds the remains of firearms, tools, furniture, and other possessions jettisoned by the hapless travelers to lighten their wagons.

Against the western slope of the Oquirrh (o-ker) Mountains, shade trees, and old architecture in **Tooele** (too-WILL-uh) offer a respite from the hard light of lakeside flatlands. The **Tooele County Museum** *(Vine St. and Broadway. 801-882-2836. Mem. Day–Labor Day Tues.-Sat.)* occupies the restored **Tooele Valley Railway Station,** now pushing 90. A steam engine, dining car, flatbeds, and cabooses are displayed outside. Inside you'll find souvenirs and photographic documentary of work-worn early-day railroaders and miners.

Rumors of an impending Mormon takeover of Utah led Congress to dispatch 3,500 soldiers from Fort Leavenworth, Kansas, to Utah in 1857. Assured that no coup was planned, the Army kept watch at a diplomatic distance from Salt Lake City in the farming town of **Fairfield.** For a brief time the 300- to 400-building garrison held the greatest number of troops of any U.S. military base west of the Mississippi. The post was razed when the cadre rode east to fight the Civil War, leaving it looking pretty much as **❹ Camp Floyd/Stagecoach Inn State Park★** *(Visitor Center 801-768-8932. Mid April–mid-Oct.; adm. fee)* does today.

The **Stagecoach Inn,** where Mark Twain and other notables dusted off en route to California, serves as a museum displaying period furniture. Fairfield was also a horse-changing station along the **Pony Express Trail★** (see sidebar this page) between Missouri and California, which you can follow on a gravel road west from Faust (south of Tooele) through the old stations of Simpson Springs, Boyd, and Canyon. The Camp Floyd Visitor Center stocks an excellent guide to the route, which is also posted with interpretive signs.

Mormon settlers were forbidden to look for "frivolous metals" like gold and silver, but 19th-century strikes by others around **❺ Eureka** were welcome boosts to the Salt Lake City economy. About 8,000 miners once labored in the surrounding Tintic Mountains. Operations began shutting down in the 1960s, and today only about 700 people live in Utah's historic mining center. The **Tintic Mining Museum** *(242 W. Main St. 801-433-6842. Summer only)* leaves a telephone number posted on the door to call if it's closed—and you should, because the exhibits are engaging. You'll be admitted to the upstairs of the century-old city hall and adjoining railroad depot, which went up in 1926. There are plenty of minerals on display, along with equipment used to assay ore.

Named for French explorer Etienne Provot, who accompanied trappers into the area in 1825, **❻ Provo★★** is Utah's second largest city, founded in 1849 by a colony of 30 Mormon families who built a stockade on the south bank of the Provo River. To enter Provo, leave I-15 and follow US 189 (University Avenue) north to two of Utah's prettiest buildings. The **Utah County Courthouse★** *(51 S. University Ave. 801-370-8393. Mon.-Fri.)* dates only from the 1920s, but its Greek Revival details exude timeless classical beauty. Inside, checkerboard marble floors, a lushly painted dome, and gleaming woodwork create a serene air. If you visit when the front doors are locked, walk

Frontier Legend

The Pony Express was launched by three wagon freighters seeking a federal mail contract by proving that a central cross-country courier route was faster than the Butterfield Overland Stage, which took three weeks to carry a letter from Missouri to California via New Mexico and Arizona. On April 3, 1860, single riders left both St. Joseph and San Francisco. Each had 39 riders waiting ahead, ready to grab the mail pouch for an average 70-mile, seven-horse leg of the ten-day trip. The operation involved 157 stations, corralling 400 horses to serve 80 riders along the 1,840-mile route. Rough terrain brought injury, hostile Indians, and worse. Though well run, the scheme lost money. On October 24, 1861, the first transcontinental telegraph message put the Pony Express out of business after only 18 months—long enough, however, to create an enduring legend.

around the building to the **Utah County Travel Council Visitor Center** *(45 E. 100 South St. 801-370-8393 or 800-222-UTAH)*. Don't leave without a copy of the *Utah County Seven Day Weekend,* an excellent briefing on local doings.

The nearby **Provo Tabernacle**★ *(100 University South. 801-370-6655)* is considered by some to be one of Utah's most striking Mormon buildings. Inside you'll find lovely stained-glass windows and masterful woodwork, the triumph of almost 15 years of labor, beginning in 1883.

Old mine frame, Eureka

The original colonists' riverside stockade was soon relocated to higher ground, where a copy of the second fort is preserved at **North Park** *(500 West and 600 North Sts. 801-379-6600)*. The **Pioneer Memorial Building** *(801-379-6609. June-Sept. Mon.-Sat., Oct.-May Thurs. only)* here offers an interesting display of pioneer and Indian artifacts. **Old Fort Utah** *(200 N. 2050 West Street)* is a re-creation of the settlers' first bastion.

From University Avenue downtown, turn east onto 2330 North and follow signs to the single-spired **Provo Temple** on Temple View Drive. After a look, backtrack partway and turn left onto Provo Canyon Road, which skirts the western boundary of **Brigham Young University (BYU)**★ *(801-378-4636)*. Provo's heart and soul, BYU is an academic, athletic, cultural, and scientific over-achiever that is one of the most academically-diverse universities in America, with 166 undergraduate subject

17

Autumn color near Payson

areas and 104 graduate programs. About 99 percent of its 31,500 students are Mormon, hewing to the church-sponsored university's moral code requiring academic honesty and eschewing alcohol, coffee, tobacco, drugs, "inappropriate" dress and grooming, and sexual relations outside marriage. Turn left onto 1230 North Street and follow it toward the campus center, as it becomes Campus Drive. Watch for signs to the **Visitor Center** *(801-378-4678. Mon.-Fri. Tours at 11 a.m., 2 p.m., and by appt.)*, where you can park and pick up maps and information, or join a tour of the campus.

Nineteenth- and twentieth-century American art holds center stage in the nearby **Museum of Art**★ *(801-378-2787. Mon.-Sat.)*. The museum café is a clean, well-lighted place to reflect on the meaning of art over a good sandwich. Loftier views, if not thoughts, are possible from the restaurant atop BYU's six-story student union, the **Wilkinson Center** *(801-378-2049. Mon.-Fri.)*.

Auto touring increases your familiarity with terms like "diorama," several of which you'll find at the **Monte L. Bean Life Science Museum** *(801-378-5051. Mon.-Sat.)*, behind the sonorous 97-foot **Carillon Bell Tower.** You could spend the day here, or narrow your focus to the superbly designed Utah wildlife dioramas depicting natural habitats.

The university's **Museum of People and Cultures**★ *(700 N. 100 East St. 801-378-6112. Mon.-Fri.)* has an unusual collection of rare artifacts from pre-historic Native Americans, who migrated into the Great Basin some 10,000 years ago. To visit, go down Provo Canyon Road, merge with University Avenue, turn left at 800 North and then right onto 100 East. Look for the museum amid a block of student houses.

Five blocks away there's anthropology of a different sort at the **McCurdy Historical Doll Museum**★★ *(246 N.*

18

Downtown Provo

100 East St. 801-377-9935. Tues.-Sat.; adm. fee). In addition to the 3,000 dolls on permanent display, each month brings miniature pageants created by the curators and depicting such things as historical eras or clothing styles from remote points of the compass.

For a taste of the wild country and pastoral scenery that makes Provo an ideal home for outdoor enthusiasts, continue on University Avenue until it becomes **Provo Canyon Parkway**★★ *(US 189)*. This leads into the **Wasatch Range** and **Uinta National Forest** *(801-377-5780)*. The highway skirts the Provo River through **Heber Valley**★★, dotted with public picnic spots and campgrounds and known for good trout fishing. Barely four miles from town you'll come to the lovely **Bridal Veil Falls**★, a plunging, two-tiered drop to a popular fishing spot.

Bridal Veil Falls, east of Provo

People used to call mountain-ringed Heber Valley the Switzerland of America. The 11,750-foot **Mount Timpanogos** to the north and 11,068-foot **Provo Peak** to the east are reminiscent of the Alps, but settlement has diminished the valley's bucolic character. Not so along the scenic 20-mile **Alpine Loop Road** *(Utah 92)*, connecting Provo Canyon with American Fork Canyon.

Continue on Utah 92 to **❼ Timpanogos Cave National Monument**★ *(801-756-5238 or 756-0351. Mid-May–mid-Sept.; adm. fee)*, a trio of small limestone caves in which multicolored crystals grow horizontally in coral-like formations called helictites. The well-lit caves run for about 1,800 feet inside Mount Timpanogos, linked by man-made tunnels that permit continuous exploration. The cave entrance is a strenuous 1.5-mile uphill walk from the monument's roadside headquarters. Tours are limited to 20, take about three hours, and are often sold out in advance, so call ahead to reserve a spot. Bring walking shoes and warm clothing—the caves are a damp and chilly 45°F. If you don't have time for a tour, catch the 20-minute video at the Visitor Center, which shows some of the highlights of the drippy, still forming caves. Unfortunately, their contours prevent wheelchair access, but everyone can enjoy the tree-shaded **Swinging Bridge Picnic Area,** a quarter mile from the Visitor Center.

● 300 miles ● 2 to 4 days ● Spring through autumn ● Good roads throughout. Winter snow can close roads in the Bear Lake region.

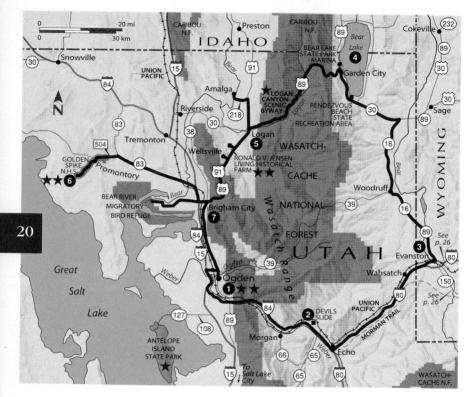

See p. 26

See p. 26

In 1869 the completion of the transcontinental railroad at Promontory Summit near the Great Salt Lake turned Ogden into one of the West's leading shipping centers. It was a stroke of fortune never imagined by the mountain men who trapped beaver along its rivers in the 1820s or the mid-19th-century Mormon colonists who nearly failed to survive here. This route begins in Ogden, then moves east of the Wasatch Range, where rural isolation prevails in a region of far-flung ranches and farms. The drive then loops north to where huge Bear Lake and Utah's timbered high country attract outdoor recreation enthusiasts. To the west, bucolic Cache Valley still has places where time seems to have stopped early in the century, including a farm stuck in the year 1917.

Utah's third largest metropolitan area, ❶ **Ogden★★** is where, in 1845, a trapper named Miles Goodyear built a log stockade and trading post alongside a braided river delta, establishing his claim as Utah's first permanent Anglo-American resident. A colony of Mormons arrived two years later and struggled through flooding and prickly relations with Indians. The railroad's arrival transformed Ogden into one of the West's key rail hubs, with traffic peaking at over a hundred trains a day.

In 1924 the Union Pacific built Ogden's elegant mission revival **Union Station** *(2501 Wall Ave.)*, which still serves Amtrak and houses the city's **Visitor Information Center** *(801-629-8288 or 800-ALL-UTAH. Mon.-Sat. in summer, Mon.-Fri. rest of year)*. Stop by and pick up a free brochure on area walking tours. The depot also holds a cluster of museums *(801-629-8535. Mon.-Sat.)* open for the price of a single admission. One, the **Ogden Railway Museum,** is a model train buff's paradise, where the miniatures rattle around a diorama representing stretches of the original 1,776-mile transcontinental route between Omaha and Sacramento. Utah's unusual concentration of exposed

fossil-rich sediments from the dinosaur age adds interest to the adjoining **Natural History Museum,** which also shows off the state's mineral wealth.

In 1851 gunsmith Jonathan Browning opened shop in Odgen, beginning a three-

Union Station, Ogden

generation dynasty of firearms manufacturers who designed everything from the semiautomatic Colt .45 pistol to the Browning automatic rifle of World War II. The Brownings were among America's most commercially successful inventors, and their sketches, drawings, and prototypes, exhibited in the **Val Browning Firearms Museum** upstairs, capture the attention of those not usually interested in weaponry.

Next, stroll east on **Historic 25th Street.** The redbrick 19th-century mercantile area is the heart of Ogden's ambitious downtown restoration. Highlights include the striking art deco **Municipal Building** and the refurbished

century-old Renaissance Revival **Radisson Suite Hotel**
(Both at 25th St. and Washington Blvd.); the elaborately decorated 1924 **Egyptian Theater** *(One block N on Wash. Blvd.)*;
and the federal revival **Post Office** *(24th St. and Grant Ave.)*.

To appreciate how hard-won all this civility is, visit the
Daughters of Utah Pioneers Museum★ *(2148 Grant Ave.
801-621-5224. Mid-May–mid-Sept. Mon.-Sat.)*. The 1902 brick
Gothic-style Weber Stake Relief Society Building alone is
worth a visit. Also of interest is Miles Goodyear's log cabin,
reassembled here. Artifacts from the settlement era include
a remarkable collection of 19th-century photographs.

It's a bit of a walk (or a short drive) to **Temple Square**
(350 22nd St. 801-621-6880. Daily, tours by appt.), where a
high gold steeple crowns the 283-room **Ogden Temple** of
the Church of Jesus Christ of Latter-day Saints. Dedicated
in 1972, the temple is closed to all but church members,
but you can tour its landscaped grounds. The nearby
Tabernacle, open to all, features the elaborate interior
woodwork characterizing Mormon churches.

For a lovely respite, walk along the leafy 3.1-mile
Ogden River Parkway. The greenbelt follows the river
through the city from the downtown area to the mouth of
Ogden Canyon, passing **George S. Eccles Dinosaur Park**
(1544 E. Park Blvd. 801-393-DINO. Apr.-Nov.; adm. fee), where
some 115 models of the fearsome beasts stalk through
the shrubbery. The museum is a scientific scrapbook of
plants, animals, and volcanic geology of the Cretaceous,
Jurassic, and Triassic periods.

Painstaking attention to historical accuracy re-created
Goodyear's riverside bastion at **Fort Buenaventura State
Park**★ *(2450 A Ave. 801-621-4808. April-Nov.; adm. fee)*.
Perfect copies of the trader's three cabins and stockade
were built using the construction methods and hand tools
of 1845. If you've ever wondered what frontier trading
posts traded, check the 19th-century stock on the shelves.

I-84 follows the Union Pacific Railroad and the Weber
River east into the **Wasatch Range,** through such farming
towns as Morgan. The roadside rest stop near ❷ **Devils
Slide** affords a good look at the narrow slot formed by
two uptilted limestone ridges alongside the Weber.

From **Echo,** a vintage rail junction dating before
Golden Spike days, I-80 parallels the Union Pacific route
through Echo Canyon—a stretch of the old covered
wagon-era **Mormon Trail** that forks away east at sleepy

Antelope Island ☆

If you look southwest from
Ogden's shore across the
Great Salt Lake, you'll see
28,000-acre **Antelope
Island State Park** *(801-
773-2941. Adm. fee)*, the
biggest of ten isles rising
from the briny pond
and Utah's largest
state park—roughly
twice the area of Manhat-
tan. Take I-15 south to Utah
108 and 127 west along
the 7-mile causeway.
On the island the pave-
ment leads west along the
shore to **Egg Island
Overlook,** a nesting area
for migratory waterbirds.
To experience the extraordinary buoyancy produced
by the lake's eye-burning
salinity (exceeded only by
the Dead Sea), take a dip
at **Bridger Bay.** The drive
southwest to 4,785-foot
Buffalo Point Overlook
ends at a little café with
long views in every
direction.

22

Antelope Island State Park

Wahsatch. The scenic drive from ❸ **Evanston,** Wyoming, back into Utah via Wyo. 89 and Utah 16 is accented by the serene isolation of the ranches and farmsteads strung out along the marshy **Bear River Basin.**

Some 28,000 years ago, an earthquake left a fault basin that filled with runoff to create 70,000-acre ❹ **Bear Lake,** one of Utah's most popular fishing and boating spots. A high concentration of suspended carbonite particles from dissolved limestone make the lake a vivid turquoise. At nearly 6,000 feet, winter snows from October to April open the sprawling **Rendezvous Beach State Recreation Area** campground to snowmobiling in nearby **Bear Lake State Park** *(801-946-3343. Adm. fee)*. In other seasons, sandy beaches and campsites shaded by willow and cottonwood make Big Creek Campground an ideal place for a picnic. Bear Lake State Park Marina, 2 miles north of Garden City, is open year-round. Stop by the Visitor Center for information about biking and hiking trails, fishing regulations, and birdwatching.

The forested **Logan Canyon Scenic Byway★** along the Logan River between Garden City and Logan offers many opportunities to camp and hike in the million-plus acres of **Wasatch-Cache National Forest** *(Logan Ranger District 801-524-5030)*. Mountain-ringed **Cache Valley** is named for holes called caches, where trappers stockpiled beaver pelts in the 1820s. The basin is famed for cheese-making, centered in little **Amalga,** north on Utah 218.

In 1856 Mormons interested in agriculture founded ❺ **Logan.** The **Daughters of Utah Pioneers Museum** *(160 N. Main St. 801-752-5139, June-Sept. Mon.-Fri., Oct.-May by appt.)* shares an old redbrick courthouse with Logan's

Cattle ranch along Bear Lake

Visitor Center *(801-752-2161 or 800-882-4433).* Most of the history chronicled here concerns the Mormon town-building movement, which established some 500 communities. An unusual collection of antique musical instruments reflects the Mormons' tradition of family musicmaking. Volunteer docents regularly demonstrate such old-time skills as wool carding, spinning, and dying.

Old buildings of brick and stone and landscaped grounds give **Utah State University (USU)** *(5th North and 7th East Sts. 801-797-1158)* a quintessentially collegiate air. Leave your car at the visitor parking terrace, pick up a map at the adjoining information center, and head for **Old Main,** built in 1889 by an architect who knew how to ensure alma mater chauvinism. The adjacent campanile owes its design to a bell tower in Venice, Italy.

The permanent collection of USU's **Nora Eccles Harrison Museum of Art** *(650 N. 1100 East St. 801-797-1414. Tues.-Sun.)* is especially strong in 20th-century paintings and ceramics, including Native American works.

In 1877 Brigham Young selected the site for the castlelike gray limestone **Logan Mormon Temple** *(175 N. 300 East St. 801-752-3611),* but it took seven years of labor by 25,000 volunteers to complete the twin-towered church. Tour the surrounding neighborhood, where imposing antique homes, regal as stone lions, sit on sweeping lawns. The plainer lines of the **Logan Mormon Tabernacle** *(Main and Center Sts. 801-755-5598. Mon.-Fri.)* represent an earlier style of Mormon church building. The impeccably crafted interior woodwork was completed in 1891, a perfect sounding board to the pipe organ, installed in 1908.

Northeastern Utah's pioneer saga lives on near rural **Wellsville** at USU's **Ronald V. Jensen Living Historical Farm★★** *(US 89/91. 801-245-4064. June-Aug. Tues.-Sat.; adm. fee).* Thirteen old farm buildings moved from other parts of the Cache Valley re-create the look of a Mormon homestead circa 1917. Students operate the 120-acre patchwork of fields, meadows, orchards, and gardens while acting as interpreters. Dressed in period clothing, they use old-time farm implements to till the soil, shear sheep, thresh grain, press cider, and demonstrate other farming skills—part of a master's degree program to prepare them for employment as interpreters in parks and living history museums around the country.

The first rails to link the Atlantic and Pacific coasts on May 10, 1869, at Promontory were pulled up for scrap during World War II. The two locomotives that met face-to-face on that historic day perished in early 20th-century wrecking yards. Today, however, reproductions of the Central Pacific's *Jupiter* and the Union Pacific's 119 chuff along a commemorative 1.7-mile track at ❻ **Golden Spike National Historic Site★★** *(Utah 83. 801-471-2209. May–mid-Oct.; adm. fee)* to reenact the completion of the 1,776-mile track between California and Nebraska. If the engines aren't running, ask to see the sheds where they winter. Historic documents and photographs in the Visitor Center document the feat that thrilled the nation, but your imagination will do a better job if you drive west 8 miles on the road paralleling the one-way **Promontory Trail★★**, which returns to the Visitor Center via the original railbed over filled-in gullies and through cuts in the terrain. The tour is enhanced with a copy of the *Promontory Trail* guide.

Utah 83 leads back to ❼ **Brigham City** *(Visitor Center 801-723-3931)*, whose Main Street passes through a neighborhood of stately homes to a downtown area unusually rich in 19th-century quarried stone and yellow- and redbrick architecture. Follow Forest Street 15 miles west to the utterly pristine **Bear River Migratory Bird Refuge** *(801-723-5887)*. About half a million waterbirds migrate through this reedy marshland seasonally, as they have since prehistoric times. You can cruise along a 12-mile-long gravel loop road that presents you with the primordial North American wild that promised—and delivered—so much to Utah's first settlers.

Steam locomotive, Golden Spike historic site

● 650 miles ● 4 to 7 days ● Spring through late autumn ● Good roads throughout. Some sections close in winter. Always check high-pass road conditions in advance. ● Keep your tank topped off along drive's southern loop, as services are limited.

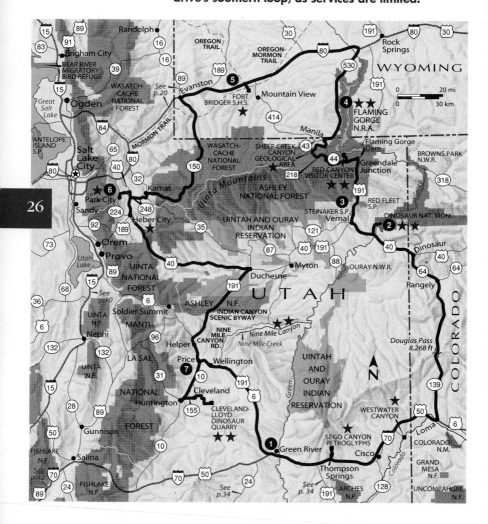

26

Farmers, railroaders, and miners settled the high plateaus of Utah's northeastern corner, where scientists now study rich fossil beds for clues to dinosaur life in Jurassic times. This drive loops around to Green River's Flaming Gorge, whose vivid hues inspired legendary explorer John Wesley Powell and his team as they mapped the Utah canyonlands. Indian rock art etched across the region by some of the Southwest's earliest inhabitants hint at epic histories but defy translation. Moving west, numerous camping spots offer solitude in wild country, and the towering Wasatch Range attracts ski enthusiasts from around the world, bringing boom days back to the former mining town of Park City but doing little to disturb nearby Heber Valley's rural peacefulness.

Stagecoach drivers found shallows made river crossing easy at ❶ **Green River** *(Visitor Center 801-564-3526),* established in 1878 as a mail relay station. Today the town earns its living growing melons. Canyons wall off the river downstream, making this tree-shaded burg of 900 a popular launching point for river runners.

Inflatable rafts have replaced the wooden vessels used by Civil War hero and canyon country explorer John Wesley Powell on his epic 1869 float down the Green and the Colorado. Powell was capable of lyric joy at what he beheld, and wrote a diary of exploration that reads like a love letter. The first Anglo to survey the Grand Canyon, he's celebrated at the **John Wesley Powell River History Museum** *(885 E. Main St. 801-564-3427. Donations).*

Colorado River through Westwater Canyon

It's hard to be lyrical about the stretch of I-70 running east from Green River across a lonely plain, but there's an attraction out here that makes it worthwhile. Take the Thompson Springs exit and drive north about 5 miles up Thompson Canyon to the **Sego Canyon Petroglyphs ★.** Hundreds of Native American rock art images are painted on or chipped into the soft sandstone walls. Three panels of the mysterious symbols and figures on public lands span at least 3,600 years, from 2,000 B.C. to the 1600s, representing three eras: the Archaic, Fremont, and historic Ute.

Cross the Colorado stateline; after about ten minutes, turn north onto Colo. 139 near Loma. The run to Rangely follows canyons of what Coloradans call creeks and most everyone else calls rivers, passing forlorn ranches and oil and gas leases on the arid Roan Plateau and over 8,268-foot Douglas Pass to Colo. 64.

Colo. 64 dead-ends at US 40 in **Dinosaur,** whose name is justified by the extraordinary fossil beds of nearby ❷ **Dinosaur National Monument ★ ★** *(970-374-3000).* This is one of the world's most productive sources of dinosaur bones from the Jurassic period. A Carnegie Museum paleontologist found the tailbone of a brontosaurus here in 1909; since then thousands of bones have been removed, including those of a previously unknown 20-foot-long meat eater discovered in 1990. Although the Visitor Center and canyon country are to the east, the skeletons for which the monument is famed lie in the park's west section at **Dinosaur Quarry ★ ★.** The Quarry Building (and a small Visitor Center) covers a rocky slope holding some 1,600 bones of dinosaurs. The eroding cliff face is a section of ancient riverbed in which the skeletons are partially exposed like a bas-relief. The rock was once a river bottom into which the reptiles were deposited about 145 million years ago.

Many visitors rate the monument's red and tan sedimentary formations along the 20-mile **Tour of the Tilted Rocks ★** right up there with the bones. The road leaves the Quarry Building and passes tilted strata, eroded multicolored sandstone formations, petroglyphs, old homesteads, and a high overlook above the Green River.

US 40 continues west into sun-baked **Ashley Valley,** and tree-shaded **Vernal** *(Visitor Center 801-789-1352),* dating from the 1870s. Today's town of 7,600 retains an early 20th-century look. Back then, steel magnate and philanthropist Andrew Carnegie funded the first excavations of the dinosaur monument's fossil beds and donated casts of skeletons to Vernal's impressive **Utah Field House of Natural History State Park** *(235 E. Main St. 801-789-3799. Adm. fee).* The museum devotes much attention to the Fremont people, who hunted and farmed north of the Colorado along the edge of the Great Basin but left few artifacts and ruins. Today, 14 life-size fiberglass models of the ancient heavyweights, including *Tyrannosaurus rex,* menace visitors to the dinosaur garden "swampland" outside.

Westwater Canyon ★

Once an outlaw redoubt, remote Westwater Canyon is the first of Utah's great Colorado River gorges. Forty miles northeast of Moab, it encloses a 17-mile gauntlet of white-water rapids ranked by river runners on par with the thundering cascades through Canyonlands' Cataract and Arizona's Grand Canyons. Walls of rust red Wingate sandstone form its inner gorge, rising 800 feet atop dark foundations of billion-year-old Precambrian black gneiss, the oldest exposed rock in Utah. Westwater Canyon was the last stretch of the river to be navigated—in 1916 two seasoned river runners shot through in a canoe—and remains a refuge for wildlife, including beavers, muskrat, great blue herons, and golden eagles. *(For more information on river running, call Raft Utah at 801-571-1471).*

28

Vernal's Mormon colonists contributed one-tenth of their harvest and gain at the community's little stone-block tithing house, built in 1887. Today it houses the **Daughters of Utah Pioneers Museum** *(200 South at 500 West Sts. 801-789-0085. June–Labor Day Mon.-Sat. p.m.; donations)*. The volunteer-run archive evokes Utah's 19th-century rural culture with antique clothing, photographs, farm implements, and other local artifacts.

Just north on US 191, ❸ **Steinaker State Park** *(801-789-4432 or, for campground reservations, 800-322-3770. Adm. fee)* surrounds a 780-acre reservoir set in the sagebrush and juniper of the Uinta Basin hills. Picnic spots and campsites shaded by cottonwoods look out across the lake, which abounds with trout and bass. Nature trails along the verdant shoreline hide pheasant, scrub jays, and magpies. Keep an eye out for bald eagles.

The campsites are plainer just north at **Red Fleet State Park** *(801-789-6614. Adm. fee)*, named for the shiplike sandstone formations rising above a 750-acre reservoir. The main attraction lies across the water: three-toed footprints of dinosaurs that trod the soggy shore of another lake over 200 million years ago. Track widths range from 3 inches to an elephantine 17 inches. Paleontologists puzzle over some they cannot attribute to known dinosaurs.

Imagine the thrill of being explorers like John Wesley Powell and his companion, George Bradley, who ended a 1869 description of the Green River's northernmost canyon: "It is the grandest scenery I have found in the mountains and I am delighted with it." The crimson chasm was dammed in 1964, creating a 91-mile-long lake, now the ❹ **Flaming Gorge National Recreation Area★★,** one of northern Utah's most scenic regions. To go inside the hydroelectric dam and see the

Fossilized *Camarasaurus* leg bones, Dinosaur National Monument

Sheep Creek Bay, Flaming Gorge National Recreation Area

massive turbines generating power, continue north on US 191 from Greendale Junction to the **Flaming Gorge Dam Visitor Center** *(801-885-3135).* Guided tours explore the generator area and cross the 1,285-foot-high concrete arc; however, you're welcome to wander on your own.

Backtrack to Greendale Junction and take Utah 44 west about 4 miles, watching for signs that point right onto FR 095. Follow it 1.5 miles past the Red Canyon Lodge to the canyon rim—a panorama of Flaming Gorge from nearly 1,400 feet above the lake—and the cliffside **Red Canyon Visitor Center and Overlook ★★** *(801-889-3713. Memorial Day–Labor Day).* A footpath to a nearby campground skirts the chasm. The short nature trail here is well worth the few minutes it takes to stroll.

At milepost 14 turn left onto FR 218 for a scenic 13-mile loop through **Sheep Creek Canyon Geological Area★,** where erosion has sculptured uptilted rock strata into bizarre formations. About 8 miles in, Big Spring gushes from rock into a creekside copse of cottonwoods. There's a tree-shaded picnic spot near Utah 44.

Head west on I-80 across Wyoming's lonely Sweetwater County landscape and cross the **Oregon–Mormon Trail** near **❺ Fort Bridger State Historic Site★** *(307-782-3842. Daily May-Sept., March-April Sat.-Sun.; adm. fee).* "Westers" reprovisioned at the trading post, established in 1843 by mountain men Jim Bridger and Lewis Vasquez and reproduced here. Mormons veered south; the rest pressed on to Oregon. The Army came 15 years later and built the fort to watch over wagon trains plodding west. The restored garrison preserves the officers' quarters and other buildings.

Wyo. 150 becomes Utah 150 on the scenic meander south from Evanston back into Utah's Wasatch-Cache National Forest and Uinta Mountains. It then fishhooks west through pine forest and grassland to Kamas. (This route closes in winter. Be prepared to continue on I-80 past Evanston to Park City.)

All those license plates exclaiming "Ski Utah!" might as well say "Ski Park City!" An out-of-work mining town until the late 1960s, ❻ **Park City** ★ has found a new career as hub of Utah's three top ski bowls and home of the U.S. Ski Team. The discovery of a silver vein here in 1868 increased the fortunes of people such as George Hearst, whose son, William Randolph, founded the Hearst publishing empire. By 1898 Park City held 10,000 people, over 3,500 more than today. In the 1960s, however, it was a rusty relic. To recall those down-at-heel days, check out the **Territorial Jail** in the basement of the **Park City Museum** ★ *(528 Main St. 801-649-6104)*. The dank cells were used until 1964. The museum dotes on Park City's sterling days and includes a replica of an old-time assay office. The museum shares the building with the **Park City Visitor Center** *(801-649-6100 or 800-453-1360)*, where you can buy a walking tour guide to the town's older architecture, including the four-block **Historic Main Street,** which survived an 1898 fire that consumed over 200 structures. Popularity means parking problems, especially for RVs. If Heber Avenue spaces are filled, park in the new town section below Main Street and hop a free shuttle bus back to the historic district.

From Park City take US 40 to mountain-ringed **Heber City** ★ *(Chamber of Commerce 801-654-3666)*, a quiet little farming town of 5,000 spread out in pastoral **Heber Valley** ★★. Mormon converts from England first put plow to soil here in 1858, living in relative isolation until the late 1890s, when the Rio Grande Western laid track from Provo. The route is still used by the **Heber Valley Historic Railroad** *(450 S. 600 West St. 801-654-5601. Daily Mem. Day–Labor Day, most weekends rest of year; call for reservations; fare)*, which headlines a turn-of-the-century steam engine but may use a smaller diesel-electric locomotive if traffic is light. The leisurely 3.5-hour round-trip past Deer Creek Reservoir through rocky Provo Canyon to Vivian Park is wonderfully relaxing. In winter, a shorter run across Heber Valley lasting about two hours is available. The

Wilderness Savvy

Unkempt and wildly garbed in the furs and skins of animals they trapped, 19th-century mountain men were itinerant entrepreneurs highly attuned to the wilderness they roamed. Among the successful was Jim Bridger (1804-1881), a legend even before dime novelist Ned Buntline's attention brought him nationwide fame. From the impression left by a moccasin, Bridger could identify the wearer's tribe. He could date a footprint by noting the amount of dirt fallen back into it, follow a trail in darkness by feeling the ground, and parlay in Spanish, French, Native American sign language, and nearly a dozen tribal dialects. His savvy could net him $2,000 in a trade of manufactured goods for beaver pelts supplied by Indian trappers.

31

original train's struggle to climb a 2 percent grade out of Provo Canyon got locals to calling it the Heber Creeper, a nickname its successor still answers to.

Heading southeast on US 40 up Daniels Canyon, you'll crest 8,000-foot Daniels Pass and veer east through a region of old mining towns to Duchesne. US 191 hooks southwest to become the **Indian Canyon Scenic Byway** between Uintah and Ouray Indian Reservation lands and the Ashley National Forest, linking up with the Southern Pacific route at Castle Gate and following it down to **Helper.** The railroad hub is named for the auxiliary helper locomotives stationed here in the late 1800s to boost heavy coal trains over 7,477-foot Soldier Summit, 20 miles northwest on US 6. Coal mining has been the economic mainstay here since the late 19th century. Helper's **Western Mining and Railroad Museum**★★ *(296 S. Main St. 801-472-3009. May-Sept. Mon.-Sat., Oct.-April Tues.-Sat.; donations)* profiles the industry in an engaging way. Historical souvenirs and old photographs illustrate a railroad lore of manly men in sooty overalls. What makes the archive unusual, however, is a large collection of rare artwork from the Depression-era Works Progress Administration, which put thousands of artists to work on government-sponsored projects.

Railroading and coal also afforded a comfortable living to **⑦ Price** *(Carbon County Travel Bureau, 155 E. Main St. 801-637-3009),* which sprang to life in 1877 as a trapper's log cabin outpost. Relax, grab a bite, and enjoy the small-town friendliness. While here, pick up the "San Rafael Swell/Nine-Mile Canyon" brochure for information on an especially rewarding side trip farther along this drive.

Heber Creeper train, Heber Valley Historic Railroad

Head directly to the **College of Eastern Utah Prehistoric Museum**★★ *(155 E. Main St. 801-637-5060. Daily in summer, closed Sun. rest of year; donations),* one of the most artfully designed displays of dinosaur and early mammal skeletons in the nation. They're arranged in two large rooms—dinosaurs in one, warm bloods in the other—like group X-rays. A glassed-in lab area permits observation of staff members preparing fossils for study and display.

Many of the bones displayed in Price's museum came

from the **Cleveland-Lloyd Dinosaur Quarry ★★** *(801-637-5060. Daily Mem. Day–Labor Day, weekends only Easter–Mem. Day; donations),* located about 30 miles south via Utah 10. Discovered by a rancher in the early 1920s, the fossil deposit is one of North America's richest dinosaur graveyards. About 147 million years ago, Morrison Formation sediments exposed here formed the muddy bottom of a shallow lake in which colossal reptiles became fatally mired. The recovery of over 14,000 bones representing some 70 different creatures has enabled paleontologists to reassemble 30 complete skeletons, including the Visitor Center's allosaurus, a meat-eating nightmare resembling its familiar descendant *Tyrannosaurus rex.* Quarry highlights include numerous partially exca-

View from US 6/191 south of Price

33

vated bones and a stegosaurus footprint. The facility has a pleasant picnic area and an interesting nature trail.

Backtrack to Price, top off your tank, and continue southeast on US 6/191 to Wellington, where you have an opportunity to view something so rare and mysterious it makes an archaeologist's heart race. Wonderful examples of Fremont Indian rock art, as much as 1,600 years old, are scattered along a gravel road snaking northeast through **Nine-Mile Canyon★★,** which leaves the highway just east of town. The canyon actually runs about 40 miles ("nine-mile" refers to an old survey point, not its length) climbing cliffs through pinyon and juniper to West Tavaputs Plateau badlands. Pavement ends after 12 miles. Just beyond the Soldier Creek bridge, look for a sign with information about what lies ahead: hundreds of rock images, traces of 19th-century stagecoach stops and homesteads, and the ruins of prehistoric granaries and pit houses. Reverse views when backtracking through the canyon make it seem like a different route.

● **About 700 miles (including side trips)** ● **5 days**
● **Late spring through autumn** ● **Good roads, but expect occasional heavy traffic during early autumn.**

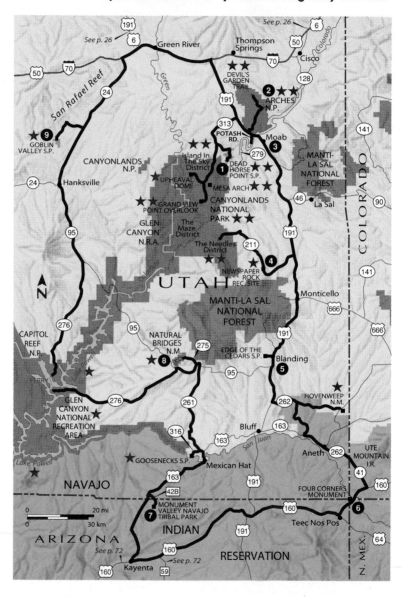

Nowhere in the American Southwest has wind and water sculptured landscapes more incredibly than in southeastern Utah, where the Colorado and Green Rivers freight loads of silt from the canyonlands to Lake Powell.

Stone arcs soar above Arches National Park and Natural Bridges National Monument. Towering hoodoos haunt the sandy basin of Goblin Valley State Park; a geological

Winter in Canyonlands National Park

quirk imprisons the San Juan River in a convoluted chasm. Pueblo ruins at Hovenweep and indecipherable messages chiseled in stone in nearby canyonlands are prehistoric legacies from the ancestral Pueblo people who farmed and hunted the Four Corners area. The Navajo, Hopi, and Ute still farm tribal lands here and sell their wares at vintage trading posts. The Navajo reservation's Monument Valley, timeless and magnificent, is perhaps the quintessential Southwestern panorama.

Traveling south from I-70, the terrain begins to exhibit the erosion that carved this corner of Utah into some of the most captivating bare-rock country in North America. Part of the credit goes to the muddy Colorado River, snaking along 2,000 feet below the 5,900-foot overlooks in ❶ **Dead Horse Point State Park**★★ *(801-259-6511. Adm. fee)*. Stop at the Visitor Center to pick up trail information and ask about ranger-guided walks *(evenings May-Sept.)*. The park's small museum traces the region's complicated geological heritage.

North Window, Arches National Park

The Colorado and Green Rivers corkscrew south through **Canyonlands National Park**★★ *(801-259-7164. Adm. fee),* merging at The Confluence and cutting the park into three districts named for their dominant theme: the lofty **Island in the Sky**★★ mesa; the wilderness of sandstone spires in **The Needles**★★; and **The Maze,** a nearly inaccessible labyrinth of canyons.

From Utah 313 take The Neck entrance road into the park's Island in the Sky district and **Grand View Point Overlook**★★, a deep panorama of red rock sandstone towers, bald mesas, sheer drop-offs, and dead-end canyons far below. The 6,080-foot-high ledge plummets 1,200 feet to the rim of Monument Basin, where rock towers rise 300 feet. For a glimpse of the Green River's placid flow through Stillwater Canyon, backtrack to the Upheaval Dome turnoff and take the gravel road to the Green River Overlook.

There's a tree-shaded picnic spot at the end of the road to **Upheaval Dome**★. The mile-wide, 1,500-foot-deep crater is either the eroded core of a primordial salt dome or a meteor impact crater. On the way back to the highway, stop and take the easy half-mile loop trail to **Mesa Arch**★★, which passes through a magical little forest of gnarled juniper and pinyon.

Entrances to the separate districts of Canyonlands National Park are widely spread apart. Between them is perhaps the crown jewel of the 20-plus national parks and monuments on the Colorado Plateau, the utterly unique ❷ **Arches National Park★★** *(801-259-8161. Adm. fee)*. There are some 2,000 free-standing red sandstone arcs here, along with towers, fins, balanced rocks, and buttes flanking the 18-mile **Arches Scenic Drive★★** from the park entrance off US 191. Stop at the Visitor Center for self-guiding tour information and a slide show previewing the formations—and put on your walking shoes. Trails to some of the most spectacular arches range from five-minute ambles in **The Windows★★** section to the **Devil's Garden Trail★★,** snaking 2.25 miles away from the end of the drive to seven major spans. Sinuously graceful, 306-foot-long **Landscape Arch★★,** among the world's longest, is less than a mile's stroll from the trailhead.

Some Colorado River runners use **Potash Road** (Utah 279) to reach their launching points. Its first few miles offer a close-up of archetypal Canyonlands rock formations rising along the curving route. Continue past **The Portal,** where the Colorado cuts a notch in the sandstone and shale cliffs. About 3 miles farther on your right, a sign announces "Indian Petroglyphs." Fixed viewscopes study a crowd of ancient stone drawings chipped into a sandstone cliff face by people who began to farm and hunt in these red canyons about 2,000 years ago. Continue to a sign pointing right to "Dinosaur Tracks." Geologic uplift has turned a piece of mudflat toward another set of fixed viewscopes focused on the three-toed footprints.

Mormon pioneers named ❸ **Moab** *(Visitor Center 801-259-8825 or 800-635-MOAB)* in 1880 after an Old Testament kingdom near the Promised Land. Today it quietly booms as a full-time base camp for adventuring, with outfitters specializing in river trips and mountain biking; bookstores stocked with topo maps; fossil, gem, and mineral shops; and Native American craft outlets.

By now you might think you've seen every kind of rock formation possible. Not so—not until you've seen The Needles district in Canyonlands National Park. En route you'll pass an extraordinary concentration of Native American petroglyphs at ❹ **Newspaper Rock Recreation Site★,** where the base of a sandstone wall is crowded with symbols, some 15 centuries old.

37

Moab Slickrock Bicycle Trail

The Needles district is named for the bewildering maze of weathered, red-and-yellow-banded sandstone spires rising above mesas and flat-floored valleys. A three minute stroll from the **Roadside Ruin ★** pullout leads to a beehive-shaped granary beneath a ledge, where corn harvested over 700 years ago was stored by ancestral Puebloans. They carried pots along the three-fifths of a mile trail to **Pothole Point** to collect the water that pools here in stone depressions. Take **Elephant Hill ★** road for distinctive panoramas and the shady picnic area at its end.

An irrigation project begun in 1921 enabled **❺ Blanding** to earn a living growing grain and hay; before then it got by as a place where local ranchers traded cattle. Long before that—for five centuries, beginning around A.D. 750—Anasazi lived here in a village partially excavated and restored at 17-acre **Edge of the Cedars State Park** *(660 W. 400 North. 801-678-2238. Adm. fee)*. A museum focuses on the Anasazi and the Ute and Navajo who followed them. The Shumway Collection of Anasazi pottery on the second floor is one of the finest in the Southwest.

Blanding has a reputation for Native American art and handicrafts (ceramics in particular), sold in galleries and shops around town. Members of both tribes work while you watch at **Cedar Mesa Pottery** *(333 S. Main St. 801-678-2241. Tours Mon.-Fri.)*. **Huck's Museum and Trading Post** *(Utah 191. 801-678-2329. Adm. fee)*, on the southern fringe of town, has a small but impressive artifacts collection.

Once you've seen the country surrounding **Hovenweep National Monument ★** *(970-529-4461)* you won't be surprised to learn that Hovenweep is a Ute term meaning "deserted valley." From about the 5th century A.D. to the 13th, the six-village community straddling the Utah-Colorado border was an ancestral Puebloan metropolis. One of the least visited national monuments, the ruins are unique among Great Pueblo Period settlements because of their unusual square, circular, and D-

Petroglyphs, Newspaper Rock Recreation Site

shaped towers. There's strong evidence that these towers, resembling tiny castles and fortresslike in appearance, were used for solar observation—a skill of great importance to agrarian tribes. A 2-mile loop trail wanders among dwellings and granaries in the Tower Group near the Visitor Center. (Rangers recommend early morning walks in summer, before temperatures rise.) An 8-mile round-trip trail follows a sandy dry wash to three other groups of ruins among pinyon and juniper. You can drive to all with a high-clearance four-wheel-drive vehicle. Before taking any hike, however, discuss your plans with a ranger on duty.

Hovenweep National Monument

Enjoy the open beauty of the countryside as you drive southeast into Colorado and then southwest to the ❻ **Four Corners Monument** *(Adm. fee)*, the only spot in the U.S. where four states meet. Many travelers assume awkward positions in order to touch all four simultaneously; you may have to wait your turn.

The drive west reenters the Navajo Indian Reservation and red rock country, crossing open range and farming country punctuated with circular, log-built, dirt-roofed hogans. Keep a watchful eye out for children herding goats and sheep along the roadway. Some of that wool is likely to end up at the trading post at **Teec Nos Pos** *(Junction of US 160 and US 64. 520-656-3224)*, where four generations of tribal artisans and sheep herders have exchanged handmade rugs, blankets, jewelry, and raw wool. Beautifully intricate rugs have been sold here since 1905.

The stretch of road across **Monument Valley ★ ★** between Kayenta and Mexican Hat is the kind of journey that sets auto touring apart from any other kind of travel, creating an intimate sense of personal discovery and adventure that lingers long after the suitcases, sunscreen, and binoculars have been put away. About 15 miles north of Kayenta, colossal sandstone buttes and mesas rise up from the sand and sagebrush plain and march toward you, glinting yellow, red, and orange against a vivid sky.

One mile into Utah, take Reservation Road 42B for 4 miles to the ❼ **Monument Valley Navajo Tribal Park** *(801-727-3353. Adm. fee)*, a concession area surrounding an

Prehistory

What is "prehistoric"? Whose history are we talking about? Native tribes certainly had their own record of the past, usually in the form of oral histories passed from generation to generation. In the Southwest, "prehistoric" implies a European-American perspective, generally referring to pre-*written* history, people and events predating Coronado's 1540 exploration. Thus the term, though helpful, means different things in different contexts.

West Mitten, East Mitten, and Merrick Butte, Monument Valley

intersection of roads. Keep going to the Visitor Center and the start of an unpaved 17-mile loop trail. Pick up a self-guiding booklet before you take the drive out across the tawny desert to some of the more than 40 pinnacles. Capped by hard rock that protected the underlying softer sediments from erosion, these monoliths were created over the last 1.5 million years. The park encloses at least 100 archaeological sites. **John Ford Point ★ ★,** about 3.5 miles in, commemorates the great Irish-American director (born Sean O'Feeney) who from 1917 to his death in 1973 made 125 films and here filmed many Westerns *(Stagecoach, The Searchers)* with his friend John Wayne.

Non-native bison, near Hanksville

In primordial times the San Juan River flowed slowly back and forth across an uneven landscape near Mexican Hat. The basin tilted, accelerating the river's flow enough to increase the rate of erosion along its original course of tight S-turns through sedimentary rock. This cut a zig-zag course of entrenched meanders in 1,000-foot-deep San Juan River Canyon at **Goosenecks State Park ★** *(4 miles off Utah 261. 801-678-2238).* Here the river travels 5 miles for every mile of forward progress.

Normally, geology changes with imperceptible slowness. In 1992, however, part of the 225-million-year-old landscape at **❽ Natural Bridges National Monument ★** *(801-692-1234. Adm. fee)* changed quickly when 4,000 tons

of rock fell from **Kachina Bridge★,** one of three white sandstone spans carved by streams coursing through the pinyon and juniper canyons here. Named by the Hopi, the Kachina, Sipapu, and Owachomo Bridges are among the Southwest's largest overwater bridges: Sipapu is the second-largest natural bridge in the world. A 9-mile loop drive takes you past all three; trails drop from viewpoints to the canyon floor and the bridges. The 0.6-mile **Horsecollar Ruins Overlook Trail★,** beginning just past the Sipapu viewpoint, hugs a vertical cliff face to spy on Anasazi cliff dwellings abandoned in the late 13th century. Natural Bridges National Monument was established in 1908 after an article on the area in NATIONAL GEOGRAPHIC helped spur Teddy Roosevelt to action.

Lake Powell★ reservoir began to fill in 1963 when the Glen Canyon Dam blocked the Colorado 186 miles to the southwest. The second largest man-made lake in the U.S., it is the heart of the 125-million-acre **Glen Canyon National Recreation Area★** *(Bullfrog Marina Visitor Center 801-684-2243).* The recreation came at a price: The nearly 200-mile-long lake drowned some of the most exquisite scenery in North America, despite protests by thousands.

The barren bowl containing **❾ Goblin Valley State Park★** *(801-564-3633. Adm. fee)* was named for its oddly shaped formations and balanced rocks that locals call mushrooms, hoodoos, knobs, gnomes, stone babies—and goblins. Some reach 200 feet, composed of sandstone, mudstone, and siltstone sculptured by water and abrasive sandy winds. The 12-mile access road includes 7 miles of dirt that's dusty but well-maintained. A 1-mile paved park road approaches some of the most impressive red-and-white-banded goblins, and two walking trails wander across the desert to meet other formations.

San Rafael Swell ★

The San Rafael Swell refers not to an ultrafashionable San Francisco-area suburbanite but to a striking 2,000-square-mile, 50-million-year-old sandstone meringue of sharp-edged ridges, twisted strata, pinnacles, canyons, mesas, buttes, and steplike cliffs. The serrated cockscomb of the San Rafael Reef follows you north from Goblin Valley State Park to I-70. You can get a closer look at some of the swell's most impressive features by driving west on the interstate. Numerous rest stops along a 33-mile stretch from the Ariz. 24 junction afford excellent views south to the San Rafael Reef Wilderness Study Area.

41

● **500 miles** ● **3 to 6 days** ● **Spring and autumn**
● **Good roads throughout** ● **High elevations along
this route mean early winters and can cause altitude
sickness.**

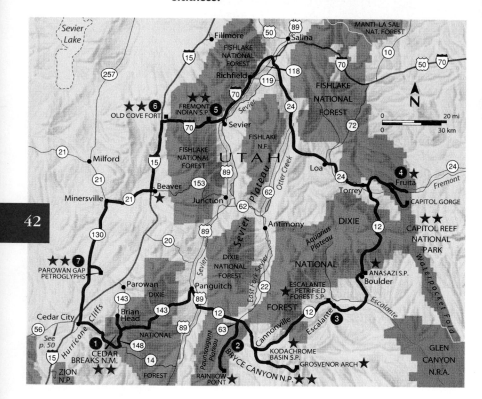

42

Colonists recruited to southern Utah's high plateau
country for the Church of Latter-day Saints' cotton campaign hoped for the same commercial success as the
American South. But Mormon Dixie is purely Southwestern, its red and yellow sedimentary rock uplifted and
folded by phenomenal geology and sculptured by erosion
into some of the region's most unique and richly colored
landscapes. The drive between Cedar City and Fruita may
be Utah's most scenic; along its meandering loop lie the
great amphitheater of Cedar Breaks, bewilderingly intricate
Bryce Canyon, the radiant cliffs of Kodachrome Basin, and
the lordly ramparts of Capitol Reef. Ruins, relics, and rock art
left by Anasazi and Fremont Indians reach back 1,000 years
to an age veiled in mystery, but these landscapes, where
their gods lived and ruled, still inspire awe and wonder.

Start the tour by driving east from **Cedar City** (see page 50). Here Utah 14's climb east up over the **Hurricane Cliffs** onto the **Markagunt Plateau** begins a 4,200-foot ascent through the pine, spruce, and aspen of 1.9-million-acre **Dixie National Forest** *(801-865-3200),* especially popular among backcountry horseback riders.

A vividly colored limestone amphitheater 3 miles wide and a half mile deep, filled with red-orange and lion yellow spires, balanced rocks, and caprock mesas, **❶ Cedar Breaks National Monument★★** *(801-586-0787. Late May–Sept.)* is considered by many to be one of Utah's most scenic phenomena. Tradition has it that Mormon settlers mistook Utah's *Juniperus osteosperma* for cedar and coupled it with a 19th-century term for eroded badlands. At 10,000 feet the Breaks have a short season—snow can linger in June and be falling again before the usual late September closing of the cliffside Visitor Center at **Point Supreme★★.**

The center stands at 10,350 feet, almost a half mile above the beginning of the Breaks. Scenic viewpoints along the 5-mile paved rim road ponder the wilderness below from different angles. Just down the road, the 2-mile-long **Ramparts Trail★** skirts the canyon rim, where bristlecone pines up to 1,600 years old gnarl out over the void, looking like gray driftwood with a green sprig of life here and there. The trail continues to Spectra Point,

Cedar Breaks National Monument

Sunrise at Bryce Canyon

switchbacking down and up to **Ramparts Overlook ★★,**
a premier viewpoint. The shorter and less strenuous
Alpine Pond Trail ★ (2 miles round-trip) from the Chess-
man Meadow parking area loops above the canyon rim
to a little pool, where you can lie in wild grass, gaze up at
the clouds, and be content never to move a muscle again.

Utah 143 leads through scenic alpine terrain to the
popular winter resort of **Brian Head** *(Chamber of Commerce 801-677-2810),* where the lifts begin rising at 9,600
feet, one of the highest bases of any ski area in the
United States. Always alert for word of new scenic dirt
roads to conquer, mountain bikers also count the town as
a prime destination. Over a dozen bike trails whiz around
11,307-foot Brian Head plateau, the second highest elevation in Dixie National Forest.

Like a master artist, erosion achieves different results
when working in different mediums. In ❷ **Bryce Canyon
National Park ★★** *(801-834-5322. Adm. fee),* Claron Formation limestone at the edge of the **Paunsaugunt Plateau**
has been cut down 2,000 feet into an intricate wilderness

of spires, U-shaped amphitheaters, and sawtooth ridges of
chalky reds, oranges, yellows, and tans. As you enter the
park, but before reaching the entrance station, watch for the
1-mile drive to **Fairyland Point Overlook★★,** a superb
panorama of the vertical erosion characterizing Bryce's
60-million-year-old up-and-down landscape. A short walk
from the trailhead leads to the towers and spires.

Six-square-mile **Bryce Amphitheater★★** is a must-
see. If your time is limited, proceed from Utah 63 to the
Visitor Center, pick up a park brochure and map, and
continue on 4 miles to **Bryce Point★★,** among the loftiest views of the bowl. A short but steep trail from the
Inspiration Point parking lot to upper **Inspiration Point**
features a pair of close-up viewpoints down into the
canyon. Nearby **Sunset Point★** is named for the ten-
dency of late afternoon sunlight to boost colors here to
an astonishing richness.

Continue south to **Farview Point,** where you can
indeed see far to the east. **Natural Bridge viewpoint**
overlooks a 125-foot-high stone arch. Towering hoodoos
crowd the **Agua Canyon viewpoint** as if challenging you
to butt chests. Far beyond the unruly spires, the Pink
Cliffs pose in front of nearly 2-mile-high Navajo Mountain.

You've climbed 1,000 feet from the time you've
entered the park to when you reach forested **Rainbow
Point★,** a lovely picnic spot at a heart-racing 9,105 feet.
Bristlecone pines, possibly 1,500 years old, perch on the
cliffs at **Yovimpa Point.** If the air is clear, you can see all
the way to the Grand Canyon's North Rim (see page 58).
Directly below, steplike terraces descend through luminous
whites, browns, grays, pinks, and reds. The promontory
area, known for its amazing acoustics, offers a deep silence.

Long-dead geysers may be responsible for the 67 red
and tan spires at **Kodachrome Basin State Park★** *(801-
679-8562. Adm. fee),* about 7 miles south of Cannonville on
Cottonwood Canyon Road. Some geologists believe that
sedimentary feldspar and calcite formed in the extinct
geysers' throats and remained after the surrounding softer
Entrada sandstone eroded away, leaving "chimneys" rising
as high as 156 feet. The park's juniper-shaded campground, set among red rock spires, is one of the region's
most inviting. National Geographic Society visitors proposed the park's name in 1948 to honor the pioneering
brand of color film. If you have time, leave your car at

the Panorama Trail parking area and walk the 3-mile round-trip trail to **Ballerina Slipper ★,** a graceful formation standing on point here for eons. For a short gravel-road adventure (if the weather's dry), continue south about 10 miles to **Grosvenor Arch ★,** a soaring yellow arc split by a supporting spire and named for NATIONAL GEOGRAPHIC magazine's first full-time editor.

Unless you're willing to walk (about 2 miles round-trip), you'll miss the best of **Escalante Petrified Forest State Park ★** *(Off Utah 12. 801-826-4466. Adm. fee).* The most interesting specimens of petrified trees found here lie on a ridge above the campground along the mile-long **Petrified Forest Trail ★** and the **Sleeping Rainbow Trail ★** looping away from it. Before you march off, grab a brochure at the trailhead; the guide's interpretive information corresponds to signs posted along the trails. It's tough going for the first several hundred yards, which take you up 240 feet to the top of the **Summerville Cliffs ★ ★.** There the trail levels, passing some interesting but fragmentary examples of petrified wood, then inclines into a coulee where the treasure is. Large tree trunks lie here, their crystal hearts exposed, agatized into purples, pinks, reds, yellows, and blues. Why here? In Jurassic times (about 150 million years ago) this was a swampy forest of pinelike conifers surrounded by volcanoes. Geologists suspect an eruption entombed these trees under soggy ash (silica), the basic recipe for petrifaction.

Entering the old Mormon settlement of ❸ **Escalante,** watch for the **Escalante Inter-Agency Information Office** *(755 W. Main St. 801-826-5499. Closed weekends Nov.–mid-March),* a library of advice on where to drive, hike, and camp in the sparsely settled high desert plateau and Escalante River region.

In nearby **Boulder,** from about A.D. 1050 to 1200, Anasazi farmers occupied an 87-room village preserved and partially reconstructed at **Anasazi State Park ★** *(801-335-7308. Adm. fee).* This was one of the largest known Anasazi communities west of the Colorado River. Ruined walls outside show what excavation revealed; reconstructed dwellings allow you to enter the dim domestic world of the vanished people.

Few stretches along this drive are more exhilarating than Utah 12's steep climb from Boulder partway up onto the 10,000-foot-high **Aquarius Plateau,** covered with

Beaver's Sons

Destiny can take us far from our roots, as it did one of the pioneers in the development of television, Philo T. Farnsworth, He was born in a log cabin near Beaver in 1906, about the time fellow Beaverite Robert LeRoy Parker, alias Butch Cassidy, turned 40 and with the Sundance Kid headed south to greener pastures (and banks) in South America. There's a statue of Farnsworth in the park adjoining the handsome Greek Revival 1877 Beaver County Courthouse and Historical Museum (see page 49).

46

pinyon and sagebrush, and one of the continent's highest. The 2,300-foot ascent begins in the upper reaches of the Sonoran Desert, passes through evergreen forest where in autumn aspen shimmer like jets of yellow flame, and levels out in verdant subalpine bowls locked in a dreamy solitude of sunlight and silence.

Dreamlike is how many remember their first visit to **Capitol Reef National Park**★★ *(801-425-3791. Adm. fee),* a lordly array of colossal cliffs rising in the isolated **Waterpocket Fold**—a 100-mile-long geological crease in the earth's crust running nearly to Lake Powell and named for the many rainwater-filled basins between its two parallel ridges.

Continue past the park's west entrance toward the eroded cliffs of the fold (the drive eventually reaches the Fremont River). At the Panorama Point pullout, follow the unpaved **Goosenecks Overlook**★ spur road south to a parking area, where a short, easy footpath to **Sunset Point**★★ ends at a broad

Rock pinnacles, Kodachrome Basin State Park

panorama of the park's crown jewel—the towering, richly tinted **Capitol Reef**★★ section of the massive uplift.

Stop at the Visitor Center *(6 miles from west park entrance)* at ❹ **Fruita**★, established in the 1880s by Mormon settlers who diverted river water to irrigate the fruit orchards still growing here on fields originally used by the Fremont people. Exhibits and a short slide show provide geological and historical background, demystifying the phenomenal 60-million-year-old eroded monocline looming above.

The 25-mile round-trip **Scenic Drive**★★, south along Capitol Reef's craggy west face, traces a route first used by Indians and later by bandits seeking refuge in its narrow canyons. Butch Cassidy reputedly hid out in **Grand Wash Canyon,** where a 1.75-mile trail from the parking area climbs to Cassidy Arch on the cliff above. Another footpath, dramatically scenic and easy to walk, descends 2.25 miles along Grand Wash, squeezing through a narrow cleft to reach the Fremont River.

Capitol Dome area, Capitol Reef National Park

The Scenic Drive wriggles 2 miles into narrow **Capitol Gorge.** A mile-long trail from the parking area gently slopes into the canyon, where inscriptions left by settlers and early travelers are carved into cliff walls. For more rock art, backtrack to Fruita and continue east on Utah 24 to the roadside petroglyphs viewpoint. You'll need binoculars to bring the Fremont Indian rock art up close. The Fremont people lived here from about A.D. 700 to 1350, leaving behind irrigation ditches, granaries, and pit houses. The carved images depict humanlike figures and bighorn sheep, among other designs.

Continue northwest on Utah 24 to I-70. Fremont hunters once ranged widely across this high country, but their seminomadic life left fewer traces than did the settled life of their Anasazi contemporaries. Piecing together the puzzle is the objective of a fascinating museum at

❺ **Fremont Indian State Park★★** *(11550 W. Clear Creek Canyon Rd. 801-527-4631 or 800-662-8898. Adm. fee for museum)* in Sevier. The site of Five Fingers Knoll Village, the largest Fremont settlement yet discovered, lies beneath nearby I-70. Archaeologists arrived ahead of the bulldozers, rescuing a cultural treasury of pots, grinding stones, stone points, and myriad other items scattered among 60 pit houses and 40 granaries. The park's museum displays the most significant items in a prehistoric

collection rated among Utah's best. Picture windows look out on rock walls incised with fanciful petroglyphs.

Proof of Mormon isolation (and near autonomy) in Utah's early territorial days is ❻ **Old Cove Fort**★★ *(I-70 just NE of I-15 junction. 801-438-5547)*. The burly lava rock stronghold was built by the Mormons in 1867 as a sanctuary for travelers between the short-lived, Mormon-designated territorial capital in Fillmore 30 miles north and church-founded Beaver 20 miles south. The forlorn garrison and its outbuildings have been refurbished to their original condition, every detail precisely as it was between 1867 and 1877.

49

The main attraction in **Beaver**★ (see sidebar page 46) are the 109 buildings on the National Register of Historic Places that line its old main street and residential neighborhoods. The handsome Greek Revival **Beaver County Courthouse and Historical Museum** *(90 E. Center St. 801-438-2975. June-Aug. Tues.-Sat.)* recounts the turbulent 1870s and 1880s, when a 60-million-dollar silver strike in the San Francisco Mountains brought hundreds of rowdy "gentile" newcomers who clashed with Beaver's staid Mormon founders. The community center across the street was once the town's opera house.

Nearly ten centuries ago, Sevier-Fremont and other Native Americans began to chip rock art into an eroded corridor notching the Red Hills northeast of Cedar City. They left an enchanting gallery of geometric designs and mind-bending depictions of humans and animals known as

Hinckley cabin, Old Cove Fort

the ❼ **Parowan Gap Petroglyphs**★★. Look for Gap Road about 26 miles south of Minersville, between Lost Springs and Horse Hollow Roads. The Fremont's thousand-year-old message lies only 2.5 miles east on the gravel road, a six-minute journey to a life-long memory.

Reservation. When you reach the Santa Clara River, take the left fork onto Utah 91 for Santa Clara and the roadside **Jacob Hamblin Home★** *(801-673-2161).* Hamblin, a pacifist, had a knack for making peace with Native American tribes hostile to the Mormon influx. Brigham Young dispatched him back and forth across Utah, and in 1854 sent him to Santa Clara to meet with restive Paiutes. The red sandstone house Hamblin built in 1863 for two of his eventual four wives and their 12 children is furnished in the spare Mormon style of the 1880s. Pick up a booklet of Hamblin's rules for dealing with Indians—good advice for dealing with anyone.

❸ **St. George★★** was settled in the early 1860s by Mormons whose mission was to raise cotton. The Civil War had ended shipments from the Confederacy, and church leaders hoped to supply the threadbare Union from this new location. In addition, Church elder George Albert Smith found that potatoes prevented scurvy, a vitamin C deficiency afflicting Mormon communities. The town is thus named for this Latter-day Saint. The Chamber of Commerce *(E. St. George Blvd. at 100 East St. 801-628-1658. Mon.-Sat.)* distributes a walking tour map of the older buildings, distinguished by fine stonework and masonry. The walk starts at the chamber's quarters, the two-story redbrick **Old Pioneer County Courthouse** whose upstairs courtroom typifies the look of 19th-century justice.

Walk a block north to the **Daughters of Utah Pioneers McQuarrie Memorial Museum** *(143 N. 100 East St. 801-628-7274. Mon.-Sat.; donations),* where St. George's cotton mission era (1861-1900) is evoked by old family photographs, farm implements, and pioneer clothing and furnishings.

Utah's first Mormon temple (and the longest in use anywhere) is the grandiose **St. George Temple★★** *(Visitor Center, 490 S. 300 East St. 801-673-5181. Tours of grounds only),* whose landscaped grounds cover a square block. Construction began in 1871, using church members sent from afar. Local men devoted one of every ten days to the project. The temple, dedicated in 1877, used 17,000 tons of hand-worked sandstone and volcanic rock to raise parapets nearly 90 feet and a steeple twice that.

The **St. George Tabernacle★** *(Tabernacle and Main Sts. 801-628-4072),* built between 1863 and 1876, is another wedding cake of hand-worked red sandstone on a pedestal of dark basalt. Deprived of hardwood, the builders used

Answered Prayers

South of St. George, just west of I-15 about 4 miles from the Arizona line, the **Joshua Tree Natural Area** protects a portion of Utah's only forest of tree yuccas, normally found farther southwest in California's Mojave Desert. To Mormon settlers, their uplifted arms seemed to beseech God as the Israelite leader Joshua did. The trees are an answered prayer for about 25 bird species, protecting nests tucked between stiff leaves or in holes pecked into the spiny trunks.

52

Hedgehog and barrel cactuses and Joshua tree yucca, near Joshua Tree Natural Area

pine covered with paint, stain, and hand-drawn "wood grains" to create the look they wanted. The steeple spears 140 feet into the sky.

In December 1873, while these buildings were under construction, heartbreak was occuring for Lucy Bigelow Young. Her husband, Mormon leader and Salt Lake City founder Brigham Young, left her in failing health and moved across town to the **Brigham Young Winter Home**★ *(89 W. 200 North St. 801-673-2517)*. A polygamist, Young installed a younger, healthy spouse in the two-story adobe as hostess to visitors while he supervised church affairs. The restored house, gussied up with a Victorian porch and balcony, is furnished in period style.

Prehistoric Indian pictographs survive on sandstone at **Snow Canyon State Park** *(801-628-2255. Adm. fee)*. The short, scenic side trip about 13 miles north of St. George

Weeping Rock, Zion National Park

via Utah 18 veers above canyons and pinnacles cut from red-, white-, and black-banded sandstone formations. Volcanoes blasted molten rock and ash into the skies here, leaving cinder cones, black lava flows, and tunnel-like tubes. Three of these natural tunnels lie at the end of a ten-minute stroll along a well-marked path. The 1.5-mile **Hidden Pinyon Trail** from the Shivwits Campground leads to slickrock terrain and lava flows.

Mormon pathfinders called the ruddy Navajo sandstone canyons and 3,000-foot-high palisades of **4 Zion National Park ★★** *(801-772-3256. Adm. fee)* the "natural temples of God." Paiutes believed the chasm was the home of their coyote spirit, Sinawava, his mercurial moods indicated by its ever changing hues of red, yellow, brown, and beige. Travelers know Zion offers some of the most pleasing drives in America—easy to explore yet aloof, and always dramatically beautiful. The 7-mile **Zion Canyon Scenic Drive ★★** and the 13-mile **Zion Mount Carmel Highway ★★** begin near the south entrance. (The park's northern section is reached by the 5.2-mile **Kolob Canyons Road ★★**, which winds east from the Kolob Canyons Visitor Center off I-15.)

The Zion Canyon Visitor Center, a mile inside the park, is the place to stop for information and to orient yourself using the interpretive maps on display. Then take the Zion Canyon Scenic Drive along the North Fork of the Virgin River between cliff walls rising over half a mile.

The wind-burned faces of the **Three Patriarchs★★** look down from a section of Zion's southwestern wall known as the **Court of the Patriarchs★★.** A short uphill trail winds away from the parking area to a closer view and a more impressive angle on the stony trio.

On hot days, find the soothing relief of a desert oasis by following the uphill but not too strenuous footpath to the **Lower Emerald Pool★,** fed by waterfalls trickling from mossy fissures in the canyon wall. The **Grotto picnic area★** just north of **Zion Lodge** *(801-772-3213)* provides a shady respite. Just up the road, a half-mile round-trip on the nature walk from the **Weeping Rock** parking area loops behind a veil of springwater seeping from an over-hang—ending an incredible 1,000- to 4,000-year journey from the canyon rim through a half mile of rock.

The **Great White Throne★★** rises almost a half mile above the next turnout. The road ends where the canyon narrows at the **Temple of Sinawava★★,** an amphitheater of colossal proportions. The Riverside Walk threads into **The Narrows★★** for about a mile. Here canyon walls squeeze the sky; you'll sense their overhanging weight as you follow the river into the dim corridor.

Backtrack to Utah 9 and the **Zion–Mount Carmel Highway★★,** beginning just north of the Visitor Center and climbing nearly 1,600 feet from the canyon floor to the lofty plateau at the East Entrance. Follow the highway east along Pine Creek to the **Zion-Mount Carmel Tunnel★★** for what some say are the best perspectives on Zion. Avoid being aesthetically short-changed by stopping at the **Canyon Overlook★★** parking area after exiting the tunnel. Walk the moderately difficult half-mile trail along Pine Creek to a spot where the views of the **Street Wall** and the **West Temple** are simply too grand for words.

The minerals and iron oxides coloring Zion likewise impart a rosy blush to the more than 2,500-acre sea of sand at nearby **Coral Pink Sand Dunes State Park★** *(801-648-2800. Adm. fee).* The magic here comes from plodding across the gracefully contoured waves—some 200 feet high. It's easier going if you use designated foot-paths, especially the half-mile nature trail starting from the day use area. Informative signs along the trail explain the creative collaboration of shrubbery, sand, and wind.

55

Columbine, Zion National Park

The wind-ribbed dunes were a favorite backdrop for silent Western movies after Zane Grey published *Riders of the Purple Sage* in 1912. The yarn was inspired in part by the Mormon colonization movement, which impressed Grey during a 1908 trip to ❺ **Kanab.** Settlers established a fort there in 1864, but Indian attacks led to its abandonment two years later. Mormon missionaries reoccupied the post in 1870 and made peace.

In 1894 life in Kanab was genteel enough for Henry Bowman to build a turreted Queen Anne Victorian residence, preserved downtown as the **Heritage House Museum** *(Kane County Info. Center, S. Main St. at First St. 801-644-5033. May-Oct. Mon.-Fri.).* The home, furnished with original items, is a monument to Mormon colonists' self-sufficiency; its brick and lumber were produced locally, and the foundation and basement stones were cut from the terraced red rock cliffs surrounding town. Other historic Kanab houses are listed in a walking tour brochure available at the information center.

By the 1930s movie crews were bunked in town, churning out over 200 oaters that made Kanab Utah's cinema capital. Most stars stayed at the **Parry Lodge** *(89 E. Center St. 801-644-2601),* a colonial-style inn sprinkled with yellowing Hollywood memorabilia.

Heading east on US 89, you'll skirt some of the most vivid stretches of the **Vermilion Cliffs.** Depending on the sun's angle, the 100-mile-long escarpment radiates spectral reds from burgundy to brick, rose to rust.

Those are primary colors of ethereally beautiful **Glen Canyon★ ★.** The completion of the 710-foot-high **Glen Canyon Dam** in 1966 made the concrete arch the second highest in the United States, backing up almost 200-mile-long **Lake Powell★,** the nation's second largest man-made reservoir. (Its 1,960-mile shoreline is longer than the West Coast.) Damming the Colorado here for water and power was proposed in the 1940s and succeeded despite opposition from those fighting the canyon's submergence. The Carl Hayden Visitor Center recounts the story. You can guide yourself through the huge power-generating facility, down to where giant turbines produce electricity used as far away as Nebraska.

The most popular jumping-off place in the **Glen Canyon National Recreation Area★** *(520-608-6404)* is ❻ **Wahweap Marina.** Lake Powell's serpentine shore-

Zane Grey

At day's end when the sun is low, the sage really is purple on Utah's upland deserts. However, when Zane Grey delivered the novel *Riders of the Purple Sage* to his publishers they groused that the only thing that color in Utah was Zane's prose. The one-time baseball player came West in 1907, bored with his career as a dentist. The Grand Canyon rejuvenated his spirit; a sojourn in Kanab planted the seeds of his enduring novel of a frail, timid Easterner strengthened into virile maturity by meeting the challenges of survival in Utah's canyon country. Grey's passionate descriptions of desert wilderness portrayed it as a wild force spurring good men and women to heroism. His worship of the unspoiled range and implicit tolerance of violence used to achieve righteous ends struck a national chord.

56

line, deep fjordlike bays, gently contoured red rock setting, and warm, clear water attract millions of people year-round. Outfitters rent everything from scuba gear to houseboats. The National Park Service has information about boat launching, campgrounds, and picnic areas.

Glen Canyon Dam probably would not have been built if it had meant the loss of **Rainbow Bridge National Monument★★** *(520-608-6404)*. The 290-foot-high, 42-foot-thick natural arch is the world's largest, able to span the U.S. Capitol. Once accessible only via a 13-mile trek on foot or 16-mile horse-back ride, the Navajo's sacred "rainbow of stone" is now most often admired on half-day cruises from Wahweap Marina.

Movie set at Johnson Canyon, east of Kanab

Lake Powell's placid surface gives little hint of the wild ride the Colorado gave scientist John Wesley Powell on his river run through Glen Canyon in 1871. His canyonland adventures are documented in the town of **Page** at the **John Wesley Powell Museum★** *(6 N. Lake Powell Blvd. 520-645-9496. Daily May.-Sept.; closed Sun. in Oct.; phone for off-season hours)*. You'll know it by the wooden boat displayed outside. Inside are exhibits on Powell and the Native Americans the one-armed Civil War hero encountered on his boat-busting odyssey.

North of Bitter Springs the Colorado begins to knife into the earth at ❼ **Marble Canyon★**—the beginning of the Grand Canyon. The 467-foot-deep chasm is spanned by the 616-foot-long **Navajo Bridge,** a steel spiderweb built in 1929 and recently superseded by an adjoining span. The older bridge is now open only to pedestrians.

One mile west you'll see a road leading 3 miles north to **Lees Ferry,** a river crossing point where the Colorado makes an elbow bend. Powell found a Mormon convert from Missouri named John Lee living here in a riverside ranch and gave him an extra boat. Lee—later executed for murdering settlers during a period of Mormon militancy provoked by persecution—turned the boat into the first of many ferries that served until the Navajo Bridge was riveted together. Several swaybacked buildings of his Lonely Dell Ranch survive.

US 89A loops around to another, more scenic encounter with the wandering Vermilion Cliffs, here rising beyond 3,000 feet. You'll climb to 7,900 feet and the forested tabletop of the Kaibab Plateau and Jacob Lake Junction. Here, Ariz. 67 cuts south through groves of ponderosa pine in the **Kaibab National Forest**★ *(520-643-7298)* to

Autumn color in the Grand Canyon, with twin peaks Brahma and Zoroaster Temples rising beyond

the alpine sparseness of the **Grand Canyon North Rim**★ ★ *(520-638-7888. Write ahead for Park Service's Trip Planner, c/o Grand Canyon National Park, P.O. Box 129, Grand Canyon, Ariz. 86023. Late Oct.–mid-May north rim entrance closed to vehicles and no facilities available).*

Fewer visitors and a greater variety of views from the North Rim of the 277-mile-long Grand Canyon—about a thousand feet higher than the South Rim—makes this approach especially rewarding. Up to 18 miles wide, scoured a mile deep by the silt-freighted Colorado, the six-million-year-old chasm exposes 1.7 billion years of geologic history, a rocky diorama that alters its colors as the sun moves and weather changes.

Ariz. 67 ends at the ❽ **Grand Canyon Lodge**★★ *(520-638-2611),* an imposing pile of rock and timber put up in 1928 at the canyon's edge by the Union Pacific Railroad. The interior is appropriately muscular: lofty beamed ceilings, planked floors, and tall, wide windows framing views of **Bright Angel Canyon**★★. The outdoor terrace may be the finest place to sit in a comfortable chair in Grand Canyon country. The lodge's cavernous dining room has riveting views of towering **Deva, Brahma,** and **Zoroaster Temples.**

Near the parking lot there is a box with brochures mapping self-guided walking tours, starting with the half-mile round-trip paved footpath to narrow **Bright Angel Point**★★, a panorama so broad you can watch the sun rise and set from here. The 1.5-mile **Transept Trail** starts at the lodge, flirts with the canyon rim, then runs away through forest to the North Rim Campground and the General Store. Or try the arduous 13-mile **North Kaibab Trail**★, which angles down 6,000 vertical feet into the solitude and silence of the canyon.

Many consider **Cape Royal Road**★★ to be the Grand Canyon's most scenic drive. A mostly sun-dappled corridor through ponderosa pine, spruce, fir, and nervous groups of quaking aspen, it sometimes opens out onto green alpine meadows stippled with blue lupine. The left fork leads to the highest (and some say the best) views of the Grand Canyon at 8,803-foot **Point Imperial**★★. The panorama sweeps across a third of the compass, from the **Little Colorado River Canyon** to the southeast, across easterly lumps of the rosy **Painted Desert** to the flush-faced Vermilion Cliffs on the north.

Cape Royal Road continues south across the **Walhalla Plateau** to **Cape Royal**★★, the North Rim's southernmost viewpoint. A paved half-mile nature trail leads from the parking lot to where a narrow promontory juts out into space, confronting the 7,829-foot-high pyramid of **Vishnu Temple** and massive **Wotan's Throne.** A minute's drive north, half-mile **Cliff Springs Trail** drops off the canyon rim from Angel's Window Overlook. **Angel's Window** is a hole through the Cape Royal promontory, framing the Colorado a mile below. The trail leads past prehistoric rock dwellings, slipping underneath an overhang to reach Cliff Springs and looking-up views of phenomenal cliffs. This is a fine place to sit and listen to the drip of springs and the rustle of the wind in the trees—the ticking of the natural clock.

Pipe Springs

Though it's known as the **Arizona Strip,** the isolated 12,000 square miles of open range and desert north of the Grand Canyon owe its personality mainly to Utah history. Mormon ranchers tending church-owned cattle settled it in 1871, building a fortified ranch around a water well at today's **Pipe Springs National Monument** *(Visitor Center and museum 520-643-7105. Adm. fee).* During summer, rangers and living history docents don period clothing and perform chores and activities of 120 years ago. A self-guided tour visits original buildings furnished in territorial style. For a sense of the isolation endured by pioneers here, climb the trail behind the house up to the sandstone cliffs and take a long view across the high plains. If the wind sighs, it's from loneliness.

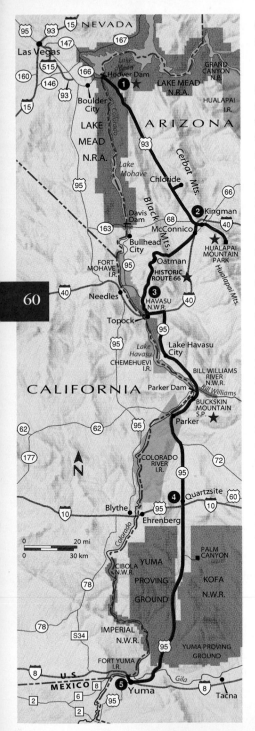

● **310 miles** ● **1 to 2 days** ● **All year**
● **Good roads throughout**

Hoover Dam is the heart—and the Colorado River the main artery—of life along western Arizona's 377-mile-long water boundary with Nevada and California, an aquatic desert playground of dams, marshlands, and sinuous reservoirs so lengthy that Arizonians call it their coast. Year-round between Lake Mead and Yuma, thousands take to the Colorado to water-ski, fish, explore, or simply drift under the seldom blinking sun. Roadside wetlands shelter wildlife; old mining towns like Chloride and Oatman preserve memories of gold and silver dreams gone bust. From Kingman a restored stretch of old Route 66 winds through the Black Mountains, little changed since the mid-1930s, when Dust Bowl refugees followed it west. Museums in Kingman, Parker, and Yuma recount their odyssey and the struggle of Native Americans and Anglo-American pioneers for permanence in this harsh desert country, so vast and empty that its cities and towns seem like oases.

It's fitting to start your drive at
❶ **Hoover Dam★** *(US 93. 702-293-8321),* for in the 60-plus years since its completion, the 726-foot-high concrete dam (the Western Hemisphere's highest) has dramatically changed the character of the downstream country you're about to explore. Park in the multilevel garage and walk to the **Hoover Dam Visitor Center** *(702-294-3521. Adm. fee).* Multimedia exhibits explain the workings and purposes of the gigantic hydroelectric plant—queen of the New Deal-era dams built to supply water and electricity to the interior Southwest. If you're not claustrophobic or wearing a defibrillator,

take the 35-minute guided walking tour through the structure's interior. (Its base is 660 feet thick!) From the power plant balcony you'll see the massive architecture and goliath generators that comprise one of America's depression-era projects.

Lake Mead is the country's largest reservoir. When the lake is full, its 550-mile shoreline embraces 246 square miles of water—nearly half the area of San Francisco Bay—a two-year store of the Colorado's flow saved for irrigation and drinking water for people as far west as Los Angeles. It's the heart of **Lake Mead National Recreation Area** *(Visitor Center, junction of US 93 and Nev. 166. 702-293-8990)*, a rumpled, 1.5 million-acre tract of basin and range flanking the Colorado River's course from the Grand Canyon to Davis Dam through Lake Mohave, 67 miles to the south.

The drive south through barren Detrital Valley isn't particularly inspiring. Early settlers weren't looking for scenery, however; they came to mine silver and gold in places like **Chloride** *(Chamber of Commerce 520-565-2204)* in the scrubby foothills of the Cerbat Mountains. The town was founded in 1862 and named for the silver chloride ore once dug out of 75 local mines. It's billed as a ghost town but remains populated by a few hardy souls who keep in touch with the rest of the world from Arizona's oldest continuously operating post office, which opened in 1871.

Nighttime at Hoover Dam

❷ **Kingman** *(Chamber of Commerce 520-753-6106)* sits on a lonely basin at 3,340 feet, an intermontane crossroad for travelers since prehistoric times. Take a break on Beale Street in Kingman's Old Town (between 4th and 7th Streets), where delis, boutiques, and coffeehouses

Prickly pear and barrel cactuses, Havasu National Wildlife Refuge

offer a place to relax and eavesdrop on the whispers of the desert wind.

Up the hill about two streets north, fully furnished **Bonelli House** ★ *(430 E. Spring St. 520-753-1413. Thurs.-Mon. p.m.; donations)* permits a glimpse into Southwestern family life early in the century. The two-story residence was built in 1915 of locally quarried brown tufa stone (compacted volcanic ash). Its thick walls and shade porches typify Anglo territorial architecture.

The **Mohave Museum of History and Arts** *(400 W. Beale St. 520-753-3195. Adm. fee)* exhibits Hualapai and Mohave Indian artwork and commemorates husky-voiced actor and native son Andy Devine.

The forests of **Hualapai Mountain Park** ★ *(Stockton Hill Rd. exit off I-40. 520-757-0915. Reservations required for cabins; adm. fee)* overlook Kingman from elevations between 5,000 and 8,400 feet—a world apart from the desert only 14 road miles below. Handsome stone cabins, campsites, and picnic areas date from the 1930s. Wildlife abounds along trails leading through pines, firs, oaks, and aspens to rugged rock spires and panoramic views.

Back on I-40, continue south to the town of McConnico and head west on Oatman Road, which becomes the **Historic Route 66 National Back Country Byway ★** *(520-757-3161)*. From 1926 to 1984, Route 66 was one of America's primary east-west highways, etched into folklore by John Steinbeck's 1939 novel *The Grapes of Wrath* as "the mother road" of heartbreak and hope, traveled west by thousands of rural folk whose lives and fields blew away during the Dust Bowl drought years of the mid-1930s. Parts of the 47-mile scenic drive stretch through the steep and scrubby Black Mountains and have sharp turns, so drive slowly and with caution.

Oatman is another ghost town that is still very much alive. A gold-mining center from 1906 to 1942, its Old West-style streets are frequented by feral burros, descendants of miners' work beasts. Gift shops and low-key eateries make this a fun stop. Check out the rustic former Oatman Hotel, where movie legends Clark Gable and Carol Lombard reportedly honeymooned.

Continue south to Topock and I-40, taking the interstate's last exit in Arizona before crossing the Colorado River and entering California. This leads to the ❸ **Havasu National Wildlife Refuge** *(619-326-3853)*, a peaceful marshland popular with canoeists, where cattails and bulrushes (the latter the papyrus of the Bible) shield the nests of waterbirds.

Turning east on I-40, exit and follow Ariz. 95 south to **Lake Havasu City** *(Visitor Center 520-453-3444 or 800-242-8278)*, where Parker Dam has widened the Colorado into a huge lake. In 1964, chain saw tycoon Robert McCulloch, Sr., established the shoreline settlement as a planned community and factory town. In 1968 he bought the 10,276 stones of London Bridge—the 1824 edition, which was scheduled for replacement—and reassembled them here in the 110-acre **London Bridge Resort** *(1477 Queens Bay. 520-855-0888 or 800-624-7939. Adm. fee)*.

London Bridge, Lake Havasu City

A hotel and marina adjoin an idealized (some might say kitschy) re-creation of an Olde English village of "shoppes," pubs, and restaurants.

Southbound, Ariz. 95 crosses the marshy delta of the Bill Williams River, which joins the Colorado here. The

63

Bill Williams River National Wildlife Refuge *(Turn onto Planet Ranch Rd. 0.3 mile S of bridge. 520-667-4144)* shelters 275 species of birds (including migrants from Central and South America) that nest during summer among cottonwoods and willows. Although the road into this watery Eden ends at a parking lot 3 miles from the highway, you're welcome to continue on foot.

Just to the south you'll find prime habitat for campers along an especially scenic stretch of the Colorado at Buckskin Point in **Buckskin Mountain State Park ★** *(520-667-3231. Adm. fee).* Here rhyolite bluffs rise high above the placid stream. This thoughtfully designed oasis has everything—campsites, rest rooms and showers, playgrounds, market, boat ramp, and gas dock. Trails pass old prospecting claims to reach panoramic Colorado River Valley overlooks.

Until the mid-1800s this country was the domain of the Mohave and Chemehuevi peoples, whose sagas are told at the tribally owned **Colorado River Indian Tribes Library and Museum** *(2nd Ave. and Mohave Rd. 520-669-9211. Mon.-Sat.),* 2 miles south of Parker.

For most of the year, ❹ **Quartzsite** *(Chamber of Commerce 520-927-5600)* is a quiet gasoline-and-hamburger I-10 pit stop on the tilted La Posa Plain. But come January and February, over one million people arrive in RVs and vans for Quartzsite's annual flea market-style gem and mineral show, reputedly the largest in America.

To the south, a display of tanks, armored vehicles, and artillery pieces flanks the entrance to the Army's **Yuma Proving Ground** *(520-328-6533),* where the military tests weaponry and trains paratroopers. Here in 1943 Gen. George S. Patton prepared his tank and infantry battalions for battles around the world. Tours are available only to groups by arrangement, but the main administrative area's Cactus Café community club is open to the public.

As you approach the Colorado's confluence with the Gila River at ❺ **Yuma** *(Convention and Visitor's Bureau, 377 Main St. 520-783-0071 or 800-293-0071),* US 95 arcs right onto I-8 west to Yuma's **Main Street Historic District.** Take the Giss Parkway exit, turn left on Giss, and follow it under the freeway to Main Street, then turn right and look for parking. The historic district's mall is lined with interesting shops and friendly cafés. For an overview of local history and a self-guided map of the city's 90 or so

---

Kofa Preserve

Some 660,000 acres of pristine desert in the **Kofa National Wildlife Refuge** *(520-783-7861)* protect the native habitat of about 800 rare desert bighorn sheep. The sheep thrive in the rugged Kofa and Castle Dome mountain ranges here, aided by man-made watering holes. The refuge also protects Arizona's only known native palm, the tall *Washingtonia filifera.* Some 18 miles south of Quartzsite, Palm Canyon Road leads into the west end of the Kofa Mountains and the trail to **Palm Canyon.** Here stand a grove of these living relics of primordial times, when this area was wetter.

historical buildings, pick up the excellent, free "Historic Downtown Yuma" brochure at the visitor's bureau.

Yuma was a Quechan Indian stronghold when the earliest Spanish explorers arrived in 1540. The city grew slowly after the mid-1800s, patchworked together from a gold rush-era ferry crossing operation and Army supply depot. The Arizona Historical Society's **Century House Museum★** *(240 Madison Ave. 520-782-1841. Tues.-Sat.; donations)* weaves these cultural threads together with a collection of vintage furniture, artifacts, clothing, and photographs. The museum occupies an adobe residence built in the 1870s.

It's easier to drive than walk to the **Yuma Territorial Prison State Historic Park ★★** *(Entrance off Giss Pkwy. just E of I-8. 520-783-4771. Adm. fee)*, as a railroad right-of-way separates it from the adjoining downtown area. The forbidding penitentiary hunkers on a barren, dusty knoll overlooking the Colorado. Its outdoor granite cell blocks, with their corroded iron-banded doors, are a modern vision of hell, endured by 3,069 prisoners confined here between 1876 and 1909. The museum is a haunting archive of prison life.

To guard the Colorado River crossing and intimidate rebellious Quechan, the Army established Fort Yuma, California, in 1853 on a hilltop across the river. The demilitarized complex is, ironically, now the tribe's reservation headquarters (the Quechan are among the few Native Americans still occupying their aboriginal land). The **Fort Yuma Quechan Indian Museum** *(350 Picacho Rd. 619-572-0661. Mon.-Sat.; adm. fee)* exhibits a small but affecting collection of historical photographs, diaries, tools, pottery, ceremonial clothing, and fine beadwork. (Take 4th Avenue across the Col-

Costumed interpreter at emigrant camp near Yuma

orado and bear right onto Winterhaven Drive, which becomes Quechan. Turn left onto Picacho Road and follow museum signs.) The patch of lawn outside the old building offers a good vantage point of the Colorado, from which Quechan lookouts once gazed out in wonder at the far-off dust of approaching Spanish explorers.

● 265 miles ● 2½ to 3 days ● Spring through fall ● Grand Canyon traffic very heavy April through September; October through March recommended.

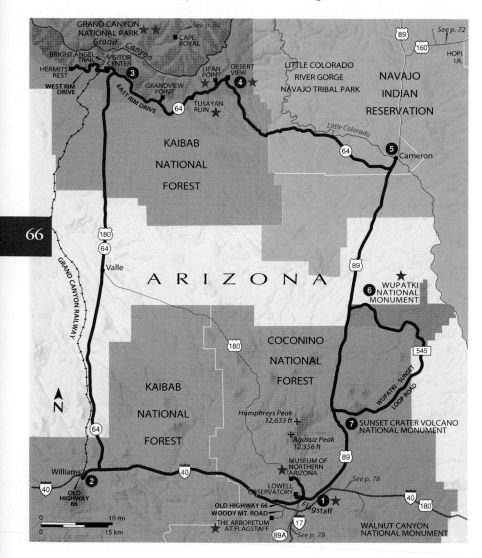

See p.50
See p. 72
See p. 78

66

This drive begins at Flagstaff, which retains the feel of early-century lumbering prosperity. Above town, Lowell Observatory probes the universe, while the Museum of Northern Arizona below examines Hopi, Navajo, and Zuni culture. But nothing in canyon country, not even Arizona's highest peaks, rivals the magnificence of the

Grand Canyon—so large, deep, and intricate that poets fall silent and painters put away their brushes. Here and at Wupatki National Monument archaeologists study ruins left by prehistoric people who farmed and hunted this arid region. Indians still sell their crafts at the venerable Cameron Trading Post, drawing on traditions older even than 900-year-old Sunset Crater Volcano's starkly beautiful cinder cone.

A prosperous timber industry helped build ❶ **Flagstaff**★ *(Visitor Center 520-774-9541 or 800-842-7293)*, including much of the elegant interiors of the downtown historic district. Local timber barons Michael and Timothy Riordan built their 40-room log-and-stone American craftsman-style mansion here

Miner statue, Williams

in 1904, now part of **Riordan State Historic Park** *(1300 Riordan Ranch St. 520-779-4395. Fee for tour)*. Guided tours explore the interior, a mix of volcanic stone arches, stained-glass windows, stripped logs, and handcrafted furnishings.

In 1930 stargazing at century-old **Lowell Observatory** *(1400 W. Mars Hill Rd. 520-774-2096. Tours; adm. fee)* led to Pluto's discovery. Today astronomers use the nine-telescope complex to study comets, asteroids, and planets.

From downtown, take US 180 north to the Arizona Historical Society's **Pioneer Museum** *(2340 N. Fort Valley Rd. 520-774-6272. Mon.-Sat.; donations)*. Located inside the 1908 volcanic stone building that was once the county's hospital for the poor, the museum's lighthearted displays of antique toys and cowboy gear contrast with the dreary old-time hospital room preserved here. Nearby is the **Coconino Center for the Arts**★ *(2300 N. Fort Valley Rd. 520-779-6921. Apr.-Sept. Tues.-Sun., Oct.-March Tues.-Sat.)*, the area's premier showcase for Native American artists. Cowboy-style decorative arts take center stage from early May through mid-June at the Trappings of the American West show.

Continue a mile northwest to the **Museum of Northern Arizona**★ *(3101 N. Fort Valley Rd. 520-774-5211. Adm. fee)*, dedicated to the Colorado Plateau's natural and human history. Exhibits in the rough stone building detail regional anthropology, biology, geology, and art. Outside, a half-mile trail drops into a canyon where wildflowers grow.

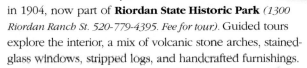

Flagstaff Arboretum ★

To learn about the drought-resistant plants of the Colorado Plateau, visit the **Arboretum at Flagstaff** *(From downtown Flagstaff take Santa Fe Ave. 2 miles W, then go left on Woody Mountain Rd. 520-774-1441. Call ahead for schedule; adm. fee)*. The 200-acre complex is America's loftiest arboretum conducting agricultural research. A stroll along the trails that lead through the various gardens representing a variety of habitats, from desert to alpine tundra, is the botanical equivalent of walking from Mexico to Canada.

Isis Temple as seen from Hopi Point along West Rim of Grand Canyon National Park

Instead of taking I-40 west, consider driving **Old Route 66** for a while. Decrepit roadside businesses and old signs along this section of the legendary highway are poignant relics of a younger, much different America. In 1984, I-40 bypassed the town of ❷ **Williams** *(Visitor Center 520-635-4061)*, replacing the last working stretch of Route 66.

From 1901 to 1968 a spur railroad carried visitors from Williams to the Grand Canyon. The **Grand Canyon Railway** *(520-773-1976 or 800-THE-TRAIN. Fare)*, fired up again in 1989, offers refurbished 1923 Harriman Coaches for the five-hour round-trip. Trains leave from the 1908 **Williams Depot** *(233 N. Grand Canyon Blvd. 520-635-4235)*, which houses a small museum filled with railroad memorabilia.

Nothing prepares you for the **Grand Canyon**★★ *(520-638-7888. Adm. fee. Write ahead for the Park Service's Trip Planner, c/o Grand Canyon National Park, P.O. Box 129, Grand Canyon, Ariz. 86023)*, considered one of the Seven Natural Wonders of the World. The 277-mile-long gorge yawns 18 miles wide in places and plunges a mile to the silt-laden Colorado, where rock walls exposed by six million years of erosion are 1.7 billion years old. The ❸ **Grand Canyon South Rim Visitor Center** *(Village Loop Dr. 520-638-7888)* in Grand Canyon Village features interpretive exhibits on the gorge's history and geology.

About five million people visit Grand Canyon National Park every year. From April through September, when traffic is heaviest, the National Park Service closes 8-mile-long West Rim Drive to private vehicles and ferries sight-seers on free shuttle buses, with stops throughout the village. If you visit when West Rim Drive is open, expect to spend up to half a day enjoying its vistas. You can access viewpoints from either direction, so if one is congested, try again on your return trip.

Start at **Yavapai Point ★★,** about a mile east of the Visitor Center. The panorama of slope-shouldered buttes and spires is the epitome of a Grand Canyon postcard view. Exhibits at the **Yavapai Observation Station★** reveal how the canyon came to be and identify landmarks visible from the big-windowed observation room.

El Tovar Hotel ★★ *(Reservations 303-297-2757),* prince of Grand Canyon lodges, perches 50 feet from the South Rim precipice. Built of Oregon pine and native stone in the style of a European hunting lodge, it features varnished log interiors and striking Southwestern decorations. Hospitality baron Fred Harvey opened the masterpiece in 1905 as part of his travel-promoting association with the Santa Fe Railroad. **Hopi House★,** at the canyon's edge, is another Harvey creation, built in 1905 as a Southwest tribal handicraft outlet. The gift store, one of the best hereabouts, emulates Hopi pueblo architecture.

One mile east, the view from **Trailview Overlook ★** provides a measure of the canyon's astounding dimensions. The popular but arduous 7.8-mile **Bright Angel Trail** winds away below, dropping over 4,000 feet to the Colorado. A half-mile east, the **Powell Memorial** commemorates the first white man to shoot the canyon's

Rafters along the Colorado River at Lava Falls

rapids. Civil War hero John Wesley Powell is remembered for his wonder-filled diaries recounting the 1869 expedition down the Colorado in stout wooden boats.

69

Nearby **Hopi Point** juts out into a 90-mile east-west panorama that includes the intricately eroded buttes of **Isis Temple** and **Shiva Temple.** This is a popular spot for watching sunsets. Westbound again, you'll soon come to **The Abyss★,** a 3,000-foot drop to the Tonto Platform. There's a wide perspective on the Tonto benchlands from **Pima Point,** 2.9 miles west. The Colorado's roar through **Granite Rapids** is audible on quiet days.

West Rim Drive ends at rustic **Hermits Rest,** where a refreshment stand and rest rooms make this a good spot for a break. Six-mile-long **Hermit Trail** leaves from here for **Dripping Springs.** Walk a short way down the path to experience the canyon's extraordinary solitude.

When you're ready to leave the park, backtrack to the junction of Ariz. 64 and US 180. En route, stop at **Mather Point ★** for a dramatic perspective on the canyon's **Inner Gorge.** Turn left onto Ariz. 64, the start of **East Rim Drive,** where the drop-off into gray **Granite Gorge** at **Yaki Point** can induce vertigo. Stop the spinning by focusing on **Vishnu Temple,** a massive pyramidal butte rising 7,829 feet on the eastern horizon.

The view of the main canyon from **Grandview Point** 7 miles east is a postcard regular. Five miles farther, one of the Colorado's most fearsome rapids thunders far below **Moran Point.** White-water guides rate the 30-foot drop through **Hance Rapids** as difficult—meaning dangerous. Stop by the **Tusayan Museum** *(520-638-2305)* down the road for a look at the 800-year-old **Tusayan Ruin★**. About 30 people, perhaps Anasazi, spent two decades farming and hunting here at the end of the 12th century. A self-guiding trail loops through the site.

Lipan Point ★ affords the best view of the canyon's eastern reach. The Grand Canyon is at its deepest here, about a mile, and all of its different rock strata are visible. The Colorado snakes around to its confluence with Unkar Creek at **Unkar Delta,** once farmed by prehistoric canyon dwellers and now home to 56 archaeological sites.

In 1932 the Santa Fe Railroad and Fred Harvey built a 70-foot-high stone watchtower at ❹ **Desert View ★** *(Fee to climb tower)* emulating Indian towers found in the Southwest. On clear days the view from its glass-enclosed top reaches east to the Painted Desert and north to the Vermilion Cliffs near the Utah state line. Inside, noted Hopi artist Fred Kabotie painted murals depicting Hopi legends.

70

Continue east on Ariz. 64 toward **❺ Cameron** and **Little Colorado River Gorge Navajo Tribal Park** *(520-679-2303),* where the river has cut an unusually narrow gorge through Paleozoic rock at least 250 million years old. Side roads lead to the edge, but the drop-offs are abrupt and dangerous. Watch for signs to safer overlooks and the Visitor Center. At the junction with US 89, detour north to Cameron and the **Cameron Trading Post★** *(520-679-2231 or 800-338-7385),* which rang up its first sale in 1916. One of the last of the early-century trading posts, it is still one of the best places in Arizona to shop for Navajo rugs and Navajo, Hopi, and Zuni pottery, jewelry, and baskets.

Keep driving south on US 89, watching for signs to **❻ Wupatki National Monument★** *(520-679-2365. Adm. fee),* several miles east on the Wupatki-Sunset Loop Road. Over 2,600 separate archaeological sites here date from A.D. 1100 to 1300, suggesting that Wupatki (Hopi for "tall house") was a signifi-

cant Anasazi and Sinagua community. Most sites are reserved for archaeological study. Wupatki's centerpiece is a thick-walled pueblo that once rose three stories and enclosed about 100 rooms.

From Wupatki you can either backtrack to US 89 and go south for 15 miles, picking up the other

Sunset Crater Volcano National Monument

end of the Wupatki-Sunset Loop Road, or simply stay on it for about 20 miles. Both ways lead to **❼ Sunset Crater Volcano National Monument** *(Wupatki-Sunset Loop Rd. 2 miles E of US 89. 520-526-0502. Adm. fee).* Tree-ring dating indicates the volcano forming the 1,000-foot-high cinder cone here erupted about 900 years ago, scattering cinders and ash over an 800-square-mile area during its three centuries of activity. A final blast collared the volcano with red, yellow, and black residues of iron and sulfur, suggesting its name. From this starkly beautiful landscape of dark red cinders, Flagstaff is only 16 miles south.

● **425 miles** ● **3 to 4 days** ● **All year** ● **Tourist season peaks in summer, when daytime temperatures reach the 90's (F). Spring and fall are cooler (70°-83°F) and less crowded.**

The past is the present in northeastern Arizona's Indian country, where Hopi families still carry water to pueblo villages perched atop high mesas. Granaries at Keet Seel ruins in Navajo National Monument hold corncobs stored seven centuries ago. Navajo families farm centuries-old fields in Canyon de Chelly National Monument, site of prehistoric cliff dwellings inherited from the Anasazi, ancestors of today's Pueblo tribes. And Hopi and Navajo artisans still sell their trademark rugs and jewelry at the old Hubbell Trading Post.

In 1878 a Mormon named Erastus Snow established today's ❶ **Tuba City,** naming it Tuve (TOO-vah) in honor of a Hopi headman. But Tuve was eventually mispronounced to death by newcomers, which is why travelers roll into town expecting to hear some anecdote about a horn. Snow's flock moved when the **Navajo Indian**

Reservation *(520-871-7375)* was enlarged to include Tuba City and established its western headquarters here.

The terrain around town includes sediments deposited 200 million years ago in the early Jurassic period. One early dinosaur stalked across a nearby mudflat over 70 billion days ago, leaving tracks preserved in Moenave Formation sandstone. For a look, drive west 5.5 miles on US 160 to milepost 316 and watch for the sign pointing right to **Dinosaur Tracks** *(Reservation Rte. 23).* Their shape and stride length suggest those of a *Dilophosaurus,* a toothy biped that would have sized

Stone dwellings at Betatakin, Navajo National Monument

you up for dinner from a height of 8 feet.

Backtrack to Tuba City and continue northeast on US 160 to Klethla Valley, then go north on Ariz. 564 to ❷ **Navajo National Monument** *(520-672-2366).* Here in two serene canyons are two of the largest and best preserved cliff dwellings in the Southwest, **Keet Seel ★★** and **Betatakin ★★,** occupied by the Anasazi people between A.D. 1250 and 1300. Visitor Center exhibits trace the ruins' human history and include a display of archaeological finds. A video tells what's known about the Anasazi, believed to be ancestors of the Hopi, Zuni, and Pueblo people.

For a good view of 135-room Betatakin (Navajo for "ledge house"), walk the half-mile trail from the Visitor Center to the **Betatakin Overlook.** The stone-and-mortar enclave, visible across the valley, perches on a shelf inside a 452-foot-high alcove of salmon-hued Navajo sandstone. Many of its original wood-and-adobe roofs are still in place. Visiting the ruins takes a day each, and note that reservations for the popular tours to Betatakin *(May-Sept.)*

Red rock formations, US 160 east of Kayenta

are accepted only on the morning of the visit. You can reserve two months in advance for permits for Keet Seel hiking and horseback trips *(Mem. Day–Labor Day)*.

Viewing Betatakin and its mysterious rock paintings requires a strenuous five-hour, 5-mile round-trip hike, including a long, steep climb out of the valley. At an altitude of 7,300 feet, the trek is only for those in good shape. The same caveat applies to Keet Seel, the larger and more remote ruin. An 8.5-mile path switchbacks down a thousand-foot cliff and fords shallow streams, ending beneath a soaring overhang of rosy sandstone streaked by desert varnish. Walkways lead past Keet Seel's 150 rooms—storage areas, ceremonial chambers, clustered apartments. Some granaries hold corncobs abandoned seven centuries ago, and polychrome potsherds lie in the dust.

When you're ready to move on, backtrack to US 160 and continue 8 miles east past Kayenta to Reservation Route 59. Thus begins a scenic meander southeast through mesa country and the Chinle Valley to Round Rock and toward Chinle and the North Rim of ❸ **Canyon de Chelly National Monument ★** *(Visitor Center 520-674-5500)*. Pronounced Canyon deh-SHAY, the 130-square-mile monument is one of the largest archaeological preserves in the United States. Its ruddy sandstone cliff walls, wooded canyon floors, and sandy washes enclose thousands of Indian ruins and sites representing five periods of Native American culture dating from 2500 B.C.

Reservation Route 64 becomes **North Rim Drive** as it reaches the edge of the caprock mesa overlooking **Canyon del Muerto.** The monument actually includes three converging canyons, resembling a giant three-toed footprint. The heel is the canyon mouth near Chinle; the middle toe is **Canyon de Chelly,** cleaving 25 miles east into the Defiance Plateau; **Canyon del Muerto** splays northeast, and **Monument Canyon** southeast.

Westbound on Reservation Route 64 toward Chinle, watch for the turnoff to **Massacre Cave Overlook.** In 1804 Navajo braves and their families retreating from Mexican dragoons took refuge in this cave high above the canyon floor. The militiamen aimed their muskets at the roof of the cave, bouncing slugs down and killing over 100. Their bones, including many of children, still litter the cave.

As you return from the overlook, bear left onto the fork leading back to the canyon rim and an overlook of **Mummy Cave Ruin,** a handsome prehistoric village with a tower rising three stories. In 1882 archaeologists searching here found the mummified bodies for which the cave is named. The ruin rises atop a ledge inside a deep recess in the canyon wall. The canyon's abundance of pictographs rivals any site of Indian rock art in the Southwest.

Continue west, watching for the turnoff to **Antelope House Overlook.** At the canyon's edge, train your eyes on the cliff walls adjoining the ruin, and you'll see the animal pictographs for which it is named.

Though the **Canyon de Chelly National Monument Visitor Center** *(520-674-5500. April-Oct.)* is located within the Navajo reservation, the monument is administered by the National Park Service. Be sure to pick up their brochure, which includes an excellent map. Check here for access to the canyon, limited to hikers, horseback riders, and four-wheel-drive vehicles accompanied by rangers or tribal guides. From the Visitor Center, the **South Rim Drive** *(Reservation Rte. 7)* is a 36-mile round-trip southeast to **Spider Rock Overlook** in Canyon de Chelly. The road winds past Tsegi and Junction Overlooks to **White House**

Old Ones

The veil of historical mystery lifts slowly from the Anasazi, ancestors of modern Hopi, Zuni, and Pueblo Indians. It is not known what they called themselves, but they became known by a Navajo word, Anasazi, meaning "ancient enemies." Among their descendants, the Anasazi are known today as the ancestral Pueblo or the Old Ones. For over 2,000 years the Anasazi flourished on a Southwest desert domain the size of New England. Then, just before A.D. 1300, they abruptly retreated southeast to the Rio Grande region, abandoning half of their ancient domain— essentially the whole of the Colorado Plateau.

75

Overlook, head of the only trail to the canyon floor you can take without a guide. Plan on at least two hours for this arduous 1.25-mile path dropping 660 vertical feet to the pale, 60-room **White House ★** ruin (you may need to wade across shallow Chinle Wash). The South Rim Drive ends where **Canyon de Chelly, Bat Canyon,** and **Monument Canyon** converge, and the fractured twin spires of **Spider Rock ★** rise 832 feet above bottomland.

The canyons' early year-round residents were a tribe archaeologists call the Basket Makers, who arrived just prior to the birth of Christ. Initially they lived in high alcoves, growing squash and corn in bottomland fields still worked today in summer by Navajo families. Indians returned to the canyons as year-round residents around 1750, when Navajo pushed west by Ute and Comanche tribes reoccupied Anasazi ruins.

When you're ready to bid farewell to the ghosts of Canyon de Chelly, take US 191 south from Chinle to Ariz. 264 and head east to ❹ **Hubbell Trading Post National Historic Site ★ ★** *(Visitor Center 520-755-3254),* about a mile west of Ganado. In 1878, a 24-year-old named John Lorenzo Hubbell purchased the establishment where Navajo and Hopi traded wool and blankets for brass and tin tokens they called *pesh-tai* (thin metal), redeemable for store goods at ordinary prices. Hubbell's carries on under a flat roof supported by beams of Ponderosa pine, little changed since its construction in 1883. This is an excellent place to shop for Navajo rugs as well as jewelry, baskets, and kachinas crafted by Navajo, Hopi, and Zuni artisans. Weavers work in the Visitor Center, their wooden handlooms slowly creating their famed vividly dyed wool rugs. Hubbell, who learned to speak Navajo and Hopi and championed Indian causes as a territorial legislator and state senator, lived at what is now the **Lorenzo Hubbell House ★.** The trader's extraordinary personal collection of paintings and Native American rugs, baskets, and other handicrafts remains on view inside.

Put your new rug in the trunk and take Ariz. 264 west onto the **Hopi Indian Reservation** *(Tribal Council Info*

White House ruin, Canyon de Chelly

520-734-2441) and past Keams Canyon. The Hopi can trace their presence in this country back at least a thousand years. A pueblo people, they live in centuries-old villages grouped around three caprock plateaus called First, Second, and Third Mesa, adjoining one another along a 37-mile stretch of Ariz. 264.

Hubbell Trading Post National Historic Site

The **First Mesa** villages of **Walpi, Sichomovi,** and **Hano** cluster atop the plateau, but before entering stop at the **First Mesa Visitor Center at Ponsi Hall** *(520-737-2262. Donations)* to obtain permission. The Hopi offer free guided walking tours, providing a personal introduction to pueblo life. Follow signs from the village of Polacca at the mesa's base to **Sichomovi,** built circa 1600 but, like all the pueblos, appearing ancient. A Hopi guide is mandatory for visiting tiny **Walpi★★,** the quintessential image of a pueblo stronghold. Its stone houses, clustering at 6,225 feet on a finger of the mesa's broken caprock edge, have looked out across the plain for over five centuries. Fewer than ten families live here without electricity or running water, which in this timeless setting of rock and sky seems entirely appropriate.

Continue west to **Second Mesa** and the ❺ **Hopi Cultural Center** *(Ariz. 264/87. 520-734-6650. Mon.-Fri.; adm. fee).* The center's museum traces the Hopi's often lonely course through the Southwest's turbulent history. Farther west on Ariz. 264 is the foot of **Third Mesa** and **Kykotsmovi★,** a village nestled between canyon walls among spring-watered peach orchards and settled by Hopi who came down from the mesa village of **Old Oraibi,** 2 miles west *(to visit, inquire at Tribal Headquarters 520-734-2441).* The Hopi cherish the belief that Oraibi, which dates from the mid-1100s, is the oldest continuously occupied settlement in the United States. Follow signs from Kykotsmovi west to Old Oraibi's parking area, from which visitors walk to the village. The Hopi are famous for their dances, among the most ornate and complex of Southwest native rituals. Check notices posted at Hopi Tribal Headquarters in Kykotsmovi for information concerning kachina dances open to the public.

77

Maynard Dixon

Few painters capture the Southwest's enchanting light and mesmerizing distances as effectively as Maynard Dixon, who fell under the region's thrall in 1900. Dixon found many locals indifferent. "In those days in Arizona," he wrote, "being an artist was something you just had to endure—or be smart enough to explain why. It was incomprehensible that you were just out 'seeing the country.' If you were not working for the railroad, considering real estate or scouting for a mining company what the hell were you? The drawings I made were no excuse...."

Mogollon Plateau

● **400 miles** ● **2 to 3 days** ● **Spring through fall**
● **Often congested in summer. Best traveled in fall,**
when foliage turns and traffic thins.

A different Arizona lies north of the great wall of the Mogollon Rim, a wilderness of lofty mountain ranges, pine forests, seemingly barren desert, and rainbow badlands. Red rock erosion is at work here too, creating one of the world's largest travertine spans and notching the sandstone edge of the Mogollon Plateau near Sedona into one of the

Decorated gate, Sedona

Southwest's most beautiful desert settings. Though abandoned centuries ago, cliff-hanging Indian dwellings and pueblos seem more at home here than frontier outposts like Fort Verde, from which U.S. soldiers fought rebellious Yavapai and Apache. Geologists puzzle over the disappearance of the asteroid that blasted out Meteor Crater, the world's largest, while archaeologists search for clues to the disappearance of Arizona's ancient peoples from this vast plateau of scenic mystery.

The route begins in ❶ **Flagstaff** (*See page 67. Visitor Center 520-774-9541 or 800-842-7293)*, and follows Ariz. 89A southwest through stands of ponderosa pine in the

Coconino National Forest to the **Oak Creek Overlook,** at the edge of the **Mogollon Rim.** You're standing on a broken, uptilted piece of the earth's crust, a thousand feet high, created 25 million years ago by seismic forces and erosion. A short loop trail to the precipice reveals the

Red rock vista, Sedona

contrasting, abutting life zones created by the rift: ponderosa pine on the plateau; Douglas- and white-fir on the canyon's north-facing slopes; cottonwood, willow, oak, and walnut trees along the river as the canyon widens.

Fourteen-mile-long **Oak Creek Canyon** ★ ★ has been called the "Grand Canyon with a road." Ariz. 89A zigzags between its sheer walls to creekside stands of cottonwood, shaded by buttes and mesas rising 1,000 to 2,000 feet. Trout-filled Oak Creek winds through fern dells to the red rock of ❷ **Slide Rock State Park** *(520-282-3034. Adm. fee).* Here, bathers slip down a 30-foot-long spillway worn into the sandstone by eons of rushing water.

Sedona ★ *(Chamber of Commerce 520-282-7722 or 800-288-7336)* has a reputation as a center of upscale new age thinking and power shopping. Art, the making and selling of it, is big business here. But it is the desert setting at 4,500 feet that gives Sedona its talked-about magic— dominated by red-and-yellow sandstone spires and bluffs rising from dusky green scrub, and the Mogollon Rim rampart looming to the east.

From Sedona, continue south on Ariz. 179 to I-17 S and Montezuma Castle Road. Signs will direct you to **Montezuma Castle National Monument** *(520-567-3322.*

Fort Verde State Historic Park

80

Adm. fee). Somehow, Anglo settlers got the notion that the five-level Sinagua cliff dwelling was a northern outpost of Mexican Aztecs, hence the misleading name. Starting early in the 12th century, the Sinagua built a honeycomb of living spaces hard against vertical canyon walls and accessible only by ladders. The ruins are among the best preserved in the Southwest, but so fragile that the self-guiding trail stops just short of entering. It is, though, well worth a visit.

When burgeoning Anglo-American settlement caused the Apache and Yavapai to mount an armed resistance in the 1870s, the U.S. Army moved into the Verde Valley to suppress it. To see what frontier military life was like back then, visit ❸ **Fort Verde State Historic Park** *(520-567-3275. Adm. fee),* just east of Camp Verde. The restored quarters have authentic period furnishings. The old headquarters building contains a museum devoted to the grim realities of frontier soldiering.

Follow Ariz. 260 and Ariz. 87 toward Payson. About 5 miles south of Pine, look on your right for the access road to ❹ **Tonto Natural Bridge State Park ★** *(520-476-4202. Adm. fee).* The main attraction here is a 400-foot-long natural travertine bridge, believed to be the world's

Petrified logs, Blue Mesa, Petrified Forest National Park

largest, arching 183 feet above the creek that carved it. Trickling springs and fern-choked grottoes make the dim canyon below a fairy-tale place. The only drawback is the steep trail to the canyon floor. Be sure to visit the restored turn-of-the-century lodge set in a pretty meadow nearby.

Continue through Payson, Show Low, and Concho toward Holbrook and the south entrance to ❺ **Petrified Forest National Park ★★** *(520-524-6228. Adm. fee),* site of one of the most amazing natural phenomena in the Southwest. Primeval pinelike trees that grew in swampy forests here 225 million years ago were buried in volcanic ash and mud and transformed into multicolored fossils. Stop at the **Rainbow Forest Museum** (see sidebar this page), where exhibits eliminate the mystery but not the wonder of what happened here. These wrinkled badlands are one of the few places on earth with exposed sediments and fossils from the mysterious Triassic period, a major transitional period of bizarre creatures like *Smilosuchus gregorii,* a 15-foot-long, crocodile-like *Phytosaur* weighing a ton, displayed here in skeletal form. Be sure to obtain the brochure mapping the 28-mile drive through the park. Roadside pullouts with interpretive information have short loop trails through weirdly beautiful areas of eroded, colorful formations like Blue Mesa, and 900-year-old pueblo ruins, including one built of petrified wood.

The **Newspaper Rock ★★** overlook offers a glimpse through stationary binoculars installed on the mesa rim at the riot of petroglyphs covering the flat-faced rock below. These pale symbols, chipped through a natural brown patina called desert varnish, may signify personal accounts, territorial claims, homages to gods, prayers, visions—or just plain artistic whimsy. For a close look at one of at least 13 park petroglyphs positioned to interact with sunlight and function as a solar calendar, continue north one mile to the **Puerco Pueblo★,** a partially excavated Anasazi village abandoned in the early 1400s.

Follow the road north to **Kachina Point ★★** for a **Painted Desert** panorama of eroded sedimentary hills with the contours of melting ice cream. When the sun is low, they reflect vivid purples, reds, and gray-blues. The nearby **Painted Desert Inn★,** a big-boned, 28-room pueblo revival adobe on the mesa rim, is now a cultural museum displaying artifacts of local Native American life that range back to prehistoric times, as well as wall

Petrified Pilferers

Visitors to Petrified Forest National Park pilfer about 24,000 pounds of petrified wood every year. Fines and imprisonment may not be the only deterrent. The Rainbow Forest Museum displays a binder entitled "I Am So Sorry," containing letters from remorseful thieves who returned rocks in hope of shedding the "curse" said to befall them. One claims that, while camping after filling their pockets, she and her husband "were the only ones to be attacked by flying ants." A distraught young woman returned crystals because "They caused pure havoc in my love life!" Perhaps it was merely conscience that led a small boy to scrawl that "When we where [sic] out West last summer these rocks climbed into our car and now they want to go home."

Moonrise over the Painted Desert, Petrified Forest National Park

murals by Fred Kabotie, a Hopi modernist credited with reviving tribal art. The **Painted Desert Visitor Center★** at the park's north entrance has a cafeteria-style restaurant, a bookstore, and an excellent gift shop.

Continue on I-40 to ❻ **Homolovi Ruins State Park** *(520-289-4106. Adm. fee),* Arizona's first archaeological state park. Site of an Anasazi village between A.D. 1250 and 1425, it also has a Mormon cemetery—the only trace of a failed 19th-century colony.

By now, you're probably wondering if you'll ever see a tree again. When NASA was training Apollo astronauts for lunar exploration, it sent prospective moon walkers to ❼ **Meteor Crater★** *(520-289-2362. Adm. fee),* site of the cataclysmic impact of an interstellar bullet about 49,000 years ago. Figures describing the phenomenon vary a lot, but what's certain is that a large meteorite traveling about 11 miles per second hit hard enough to vaporize itself and leave a crater nearly a mile wide and 60 stories deep, the largest on earth. Continue west on I-40 to Meteor Crater

Geronimo tourist stop, west of Holbrook

Old Exuberant 66

Roadside merchants have always behaved, well, let's say *exuberantly* along Route 66, especially in Arizona and New Mexico. They erect plaster dinosaurs to sell hamburgers, pour cement into conical shapes and call them tepees ("Sleep in a Wigwam!"), and display travesties of taxidermy, old license plates, bottles, and hub caps in "museums." Sure, it's silly, but Route 66 buffs say it was just a friendly way to put motorists at ease and get them to stop. Most of these places are in their twilight years—paint peeling, windows boarded up. But when driving I-40, keep an eye out for parallel stretches of the old Main Street of America.

Road and the Visitor Center 6 miles south. The **Museum of Astrogeology** here answers every question you could ask about meteors. The crater bowl is off-limits, but guided tours to the rim afford a good look at this awesome dent in the earth.

About 7 miles west of here, engineers in 1882 proudly spanned the 250-foot-deep gorge of **Canyon Diablo** with a 541-foot-long iron railroad bridge. The canyon, a deep Kaibab limestone fissure, is well worth a look, although the road leading to it is dirt.

Some 850 years ago, the Sinagua people lived in this region. Among the evidence they left behind: 87 cliff dwellings comprising some 300 rooms built into the cave-like recesses of an overhanging 400-foot-deep limestone gorge, now ❽ **Walnut Canyon National Monument** ★ *(I-40 to Walnut Canyon Rd. 520-526-3367. Adm. fee).* They also planted fields of beans, corn, and squash along the canyon rim. A self-guiding trail descends the canyon wall to a cluster of 25 rooms. (The 240-step path is steep and not recommended for anyone with heart or respiratory problems.) You will not find a place in the Southwest that transcends time so swiftly and totally as this—though the old Sinagua stronghold is only 7 miles from Flagstaff and the end of your journey.

● **285 miles** ● **2½ to 4 days** ● **All year (but call ahead for road conditions when weather is wet or snowy)** ● **All roads paved, except for several access roads of gravel or dirt.**

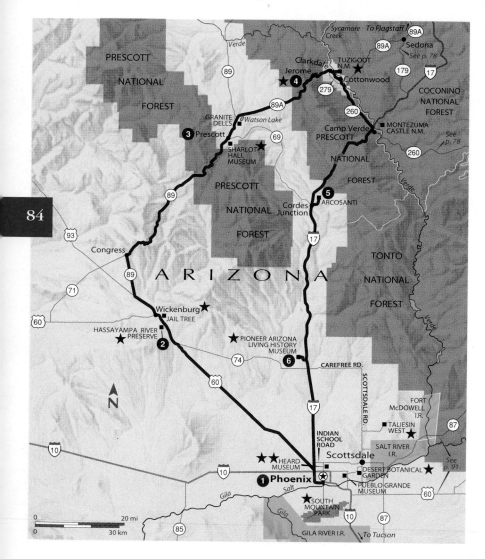

84

Thoroughly modern Phoenix reveals its past mainly in museums and downtown enclaves of old-time architecture. Adobe ruins near Papago Park along the Salt River date from the early centuries of the last millennium. Architect Frank Lloyd Wright built a winter home in neighboring

Scottsdale; his one-time acolyte Paolo Soleri is building a city of the future to the north. Gold strikes and the harvest of other riches boomed in this region, creating such towns as stoic Wickenburg, urbane Prescott, and artistic Jerome. Nearby, pueblo ruins along the Verde River warn of the limits the arid climate north of the Sonoran Desert sets on human endeavor, while old buildings preserved at the Pioneer Arizona Living History Museum attest to the ambition of newcomers to overcome them and prosper.

In 1866 there was no ❶ **Phoenix** *(Visitors Bureau, 400 E. Van Buren St. 602-254-6500),* only a hay camp on a Salt River floodplain studded with crumbling ruins and cut by ancient canals. Today, Arizona's capital city and its metropolis dominate the 2,000-square-mile Valley of the Sun. More than two million people populate this suburban sprawl, claiming the surrounding cactus and creosote scrub desert at a swift rate.

Downtown Phoenix

Gain a historical overview at the renowned **Heard Museum**★★ *(22 E. Monte Vista Rd. 602-252-8840. Adm. fee),* north of the Civic Center area. Its Southwest Native American cultural archive is one of America's finest, including a celebrated Hopi kachina doll collection. The Heard's permanent "Native Peoples of the Southwest" exhibit displays exquisitely crafted baskets, jewelry, pottery, and textiles.

Two blocks south on Central Avenue, the American West collection at the **Phoenix Art Museum**★ *(1625 N. Central Ave. 602-257-1880. Tues.-Sun.; adm. fee)* contains outstanding works ranging from cowboy artists like Frederic Remington to modernists such as Georgia O'Keeffe.

Some fine examples of Phoenix's turn-of-the-century Victorian residential and redbrick mercantile architecture survive in **Heritage Square** *(7th and Monroe Sts.*

85

Cactuses, Desert Botanical Garden

Cactus Leaguers

Ever heard of the Tucson Toros? The Phoenix Firebirds? How about the Albuquerque Dukes? They're minor league baseball clubs, members of the ten-team Triple-A Pacific Coast League. (Triple-A is the top rung of the minors; each club is a farm team affiliated with a major league organization.) If you're in Phoenix, Tucson, or Albuquerque anytime between spring training in early March and the season's end in early September, here's your chance to see professional baseball at its friendliest, in relaxed little stadiums where tomorrow's stars chat with fans over the rail, and a ticket costs less than a movie. All teams have recorded schedule and ticket information telephone numbers.

86

602-262-5071. Tues.-Sat.). Take a guided tour through the 1895 **Rosson House**★ *(6th and Monroe Sts. 602-262-5029. Wed.-Sun.; adm. fee).* The workmanship—what $7,525 bought a century ago—is astounding.

Head west from downtown to 17th Avenue and the **Arizona State Capitol Museum**★ *(1700 W. Washington St. 602-542-4675. Mon.-Sat.).* The four-story, copper-domed edifice was built in 1900 to house the territorial legislature, becoming the State Capitol in 1912. Handwritten papers and records recall slower times. The smell of varnished wood, waxed floors, and law books in the restored governor's offices and the Senate Chamber make it seem as though the mustachioed legislators staring out from old photographs have merely gone on recess.

It takes a mining state to put together a collection like the one at the **Arizona Mining and Mineral Museum** *(1502 W. Washington St. 602-255-3791. Mon.-Sat.),* two blocks east. This rock-hound's heaven displays over 3,000 samples of metallic ores, minerals, gemstones, and other precious things from underground.

From about A.D. 1 to 1500, an adobe-dwelling tribe grew corn, beans, cotton, and squash along hand-dug irrigation canals looping from the Salt River. Local Pima Indians call them the Hohokam—the "vanished ones." The **Pueblo Grande Museum** *(4619 E. Washington St. 602-495-0900. Adm. fee),* a short drive east of downtown on Van Buren, protects the remains of a Hohokam platform mound and the canals that supplied it, and exhibits an intriguing collection of artifacts.

Drive east on Van Buren to the 145-acre **Desert Botanical Garden**★ *(1201 N. Galvin Pkwy. 602-941-1217. Adm. fee)* in nearby Papago Park. Literally bristling with thousands of plants adapted to Arizona's desert climate, this is a great place to come face-to-face with the towering saguaro cactus. If you visit between late February and May, you'll be amazed at the profusion of wildflowers.

When this far east of downtown Phoenix, you're in **Scottsdale** *(Chamber of Commerce 602-945-8481 or 800-877-1117),* once the western winter retreat of visionary architect Frank Lloyd Wright. Wright combined local rocks and sand with redwood to build his signature residence and studio-school complex, **Taliesin West** ★ *(12621 N. Frank Lloyd Wright Blvd. 602-860-2700. Adm. fee).* Hour-long guided tours provide insight into the architect's legacy here at the foot of the McDowell Mountains. An upscale community with a plethora of art galleries, boutiques, and restaurants, Scottsdale started out as a destination for consumptives hoping for a sun cure. Many of its vintage buildings survive in **Old Town Scottsdale.** The **Scottsdale Historical Museum** (*7333 Scottsdale Mall. 602-945-4499. Wed.-Sun.; donations*) keeps the city's scrapbook in a red-brick schoolhouse mortared together in 1909.

For lovely sundown views of Phoenix and the Valley of the Sun, drive south on Central Avenue from downtown Phoenix to **South Mountain Park ★** (*602-495-0222*), 17,000 acres of classic Sonoran Desert cactuses, trees, and scrub brush on a rumpled landscape. Follow the signs to Dobbins Lookout, one of the highest points in the park.

Most of the 58-mile run northwest to Wickenburg crosses desert dry as a bone. If you could add water, it would bloom as it does at the Nature Conservancy's

❷ Hassayampa River Preserve ★ (*US 60. 520-684-2272. Wed.-Sun.; donations*). The Hassayampa flows mostly underground but surfaces for 5 miles here to create an oasis of cactuses, palms, cottonwoods, and willows noisy with wildlife. The adobe Visitor Center, an old stagecoach stop, has a good bookstore devoted to local and Southwest subjects.

Bucking horse statue, Old Town Scottsdale

When you roll into the old gold-mining town of **Wickenburg ★** (*Chamber of Commerce, 215 N. Frontier St. 520-684-5479*), immediately grab a free copy of the Chamber of Commerce's excellent "Wickenburg Visitors Guide." It includes a historical walking tour map of 21 downtown sites, including the frowsy 200-year-old mesquite **Jail Tree** (*Tegner Street and Wickenburg Way*), where Wickenburg chained lawbreakers from 1863 to 1890. The Atchison, Topeka & Santa Fe used to chuff through Wickenburg—think of Judy Garland singing that song in *The Harvey Girls.* During the first half of the 20th century, if you bought a ticket west from Chicago, your Pullman sleeper may well have arrived behind **Old No. 761,** a steam locomotive dry-docked behind the Municipal Center near Apache and Tegner Streets.

Indian rug, Prescott

One block south of Tegner Street at the US 60/93 junction, you'll find the **Desert Caballeros Western Museum** *(21 N. Frontier St. 520-684-2272. Adm. fee),* a rich grab-bag collection of local artifacts and souvenirs of times past. The Western art collection here is among the finest in the state of Arizona, with paintings and sculptures by Frederic Remington, Charles Russell, Albert Bierstadt, and Thomas Moran. The museum re-creates downtown Wickenburg circa 1900; exhibits include a general store, livery stable, hotel, and, naturally, a saloon.

❸ Prescott *(Chamber of Commerce 520-445-2000 or 800-266-7534)* was Arizona's first territorial capital, and its many 19th-century Victorian and traditional New England clapboard houses still seem proud of it. Montezuma Street,

Yavapi County Courthouse, Prescott

along downtown Prescott's Plaza, once counted over two dozen 24-hour saloons, and still squeezes a few friendly pubs into the crowd of shops.

Relics from Prescott's youth crowd the **Sharlot Hall Museum★** *(415 W. Gurley St. 520-445-3122. Donations),* loaded with antiques and a remarkable collection of glass-plate photographs. The museum's grounds

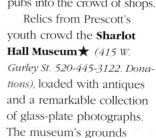

embrace a cluster of old buildings, including Prescott's first residence and the log-built territorial **Governor's Mansion** (the 1864 original), whose authentic furnishings reflect Civil War-era styles. There's a lovely rose garden outside, where you can relax on a bench, smell the flowers, and watch clouds drift across the sky—usually a vivid blue here at 5,300 feet.

One of the Southwest's premier collections of Native American baskets and pottery makes Prescott's **Smoki Museum**★★ *(147 N. Arizona St. 520-445-1230. May-Oct. Thurs.-Tues.; adm. fee)* a worthwhile stop.

Northbound from Prescott on Ariz. 89, you'll soon see massive, rounded granite boulders abutting the pavement. These are the stony fringe of the **Granite Dells,** a popular camping and hiking area. The huge rocks huddle around **Watson Lake** like elephants, creating mazes that let hikers flirt with the sensation of being hopelessly lost.

Between 1876 and 1953, the mines of ❹ **Jerome**★ *(Chamber of Commerce 520-634-2900)* produced over one billion dollars worth of copper, ballooning the town's population to a peak of 15,000 in 1929. The mines shut in 1953, and Jerome was soon 50 residents away from ghost town status. About 400 people have moved back, lured in part by the mile-high views across the Verde Valley. Many are artists, and the old town appears destined for a new life as yet another creative island in the Southwest sky.

Canoers on Watkins Lake, near Granite Dells

Not surprisingly, there's a wealth of mining memorabilia downtown at the **Mine Museum** *(200 Main St. 520-634-5477. Adm. fee).* Old mining stock certificates bear dollar amounts still impressive today. In 1916 "Rawhide Jimmy" Douglas, one of Jerome's highest-rolling mine owners, moved his family into the imposing adobe-brick manse that now serves as the museum of **Jerome State Historic Park**★ *(Ariz. 89A and State Park Rd. 520-634-5381. Adm. fee),* a short drive out of town. Be sure to watch the video on Jerome's history. Consider bringing a lunch to enjoy at the picnic area; the views are gorgeous.

Two miles east of Clarkdale, **Tuzigoot National Monument**★ *(Visitor Center 520-634-5564. Adm. fee)* protects the ruins of a 110-room hilltop pueblo occupied from about A.D. 1000 to 1400 by some 250 Sinagua Indians. They left behind an archaeological treasure trove of tools, weapons, jewelry, textiles, pottery, and beads, displayed in a museum containing a re-created pueblo room. The steep trail to the pueblo remnants is well worth the effort.

If you want to linger along the Verde River, consider **Dead Horse Ranch State Park** *(520-634-5283)* between Clarkdale and Cottonwood. Bird-watchers rate it highly; they've counted over 132 species by the river's banks.

Paolo Soleri's Arcosanti, near Cordes Junction

Two miles east of Cordes Junction, the experimental community of **⑤ Arcosanti** *(520-632-7135. Guided tours hourly; donations)* is determined not to go the way of the Hohokam. Italian architect and urban planner Paolo Soleri arrived in Arizona in 1946 with a vision of melding architecture and ecology into a single discipline called "arcology." His goal—an alternative to urban sprawl and the inefficient use of energy—is the creation of energy-independent "urban habitats" of living and working space supported by large-scale solar greenhouses. The proto-type is Arcosanti, a 7-acre community originally intended to rise up to 25 stories and accommodate 5,000 people.

Life was both far simpler and far more difficult for the people commemorated at the **⑥ Pioneer Arizona Living History Museum★** *(I-17 to Pioneer Rd. 602-993-0212. Oct.-May Wed.-Sun.; adm. fee),* a collection of 26 original and reconstructed buildings dating from 1861 to 1912. Inter-preters dressed in period clothing go about their 19th-century business. Don't be shy about questions—your hosts will probably strike up a conversation, anyway.

Salt River Basin ★

● **730 miles** ● **3 to 4 days** ● **All year** ● **Mostly paved roads; some side trips on gravel and graded roads may be too steep or curvy for long RVs and car-trailer combinations.**

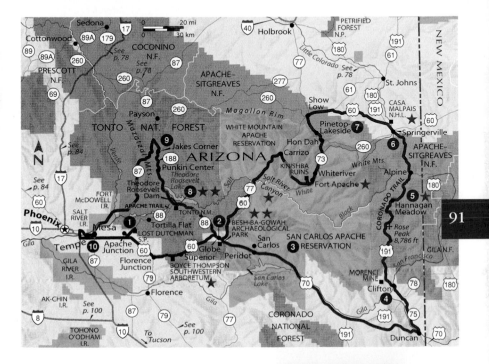

Few parts of Arizona combine so much scenic variety as its central highlands. This drive takes you quickly (often steeply) up from the southern Sonoran Desert over the Mogollon Rim to forests and meadows atop the Colorado Plateau. Among the riches along the way, the state's mining heritage is commemorated in the Superstition Mountains and in old boomtowns. Pueblo ruins attest to the inhospitable side of the high desert's beauty, while an arboretum celebrates the awesome variety of the region's hardy plant life. Salt River Canyon mimics the shapes and colors of the Grand Canyon. Onetime refuges of Apache bands are now outdoor recreation areas, and an early-century dam banks the Salt River's flow in a vast reservoir. But implacable aridity makes it likely that central Arizona will always have long stretches of lonely road.

Agave, Boyce Thompson Southwestern Arboretum

From Phoenix (see page 85), take US 60 east to Idaho Road. Turn left and continue north through Apache Junction. Here, on Ariz. 88, you'll pick up the first leg of the **Apache Trail** (see sidebar this page) to ❶ **Lost Dutchman State Park** *(602-982-4485. Adm. fee)* at the base of the Superstition Mountains. In the 1870s German prospector Jacob Waltz claimed he'd found a fabulous vein of gold deep in this Sonoran Desert maze of cliffs, canyons, draws, and gullies, but since then no one has been able to trace his path back to the lode. Many still search for the "Dutchman's" El Dorado from trails piercing the Superstition Wilderness Area. Whether you strike it rich or not, this is a lovely place to have a picnic or explore on foot, especially in fall and spring.

Backtrack to US 60 and continue east. There are laws against digging up desert flora, but just west of Superior you can choose from the hundreds of cactuses, succulents, and assorted desert plants sold at the **Boyce Thompson Southwestern Arboretum★** *(520-689-2811. Adm. fee).* The state park and preserve was founded by its mining magnate and philanthropist namesake in the 1920s to showcase the variety and beauty of desert plants, demonstrate their suitability as decorative shrubs, and identify and develop plants useful for food, textiles, and medicines. The University of Arizona conducts closed research on most of the 1,350 acres, but its 160-acre botanical garden—a songbird haven—is open for your enjoyment. It nurtures about 2,800 species of familiar and bizarre-looking plants from the world's thirstiest places. Spend 30 minutes along trails in this sun-struck bouquet, and you'll wonder how Hollywood Westerns ever got away with all that talk about "lifeless" deserts.

Continue east to the small town of ❷ **Globe** *(Chamber of Commerce 520-425-4495 or 800-804-5623),* a stately collection of vintage buildings huddled along Pinal Creek amid a surprising number of Arizona cypress trees. Park along Broad Street and explore the **Globe Historic District** using the Chamber of Commerce's walking tour map, stocked everywhere. Globe owes its existence mainly to silver and copper mining. Old Dominion—far and away the most profitable mine—turned out a $134,000,000 bonanza lasting from the 1880s to the Depression. The old post office and courthouse are poignant relics of the days when ribbon cuttings for new public buildings were

Scenic Cliff-Hanger

Many rate the 46-mile **Apache Trail** between Apache Junction and Roosevelt Dam as America's most scenic drive. It's a cliff-hanger, though—22 miles on gravel and extremely steep. But if you have the time and the nerve, continue north from Lost Dutchman State Park (returning via Ariz. 88). The attractions come fast: azure **Canyon Lake;** the cocky Old West stagecoach stop of **Tortilla Flat,** where the trail officially begins; **Fish Creek Canyon,** a 2,000-foot-deep crevasse; sinuous **Apache Lake,** stretching languorously against the colorful Painted Cliffs. Theodore Roosevelt, who drove the trail in 1911 to dedicate the dam bearing his name, proclaimed the drive "one of the most spectacular, best worth seeing in the world, and I hope our people will realize that. I want to see them come in by the tens of thousands here...."

lustily cheered as milestones on the march of progress.

In A.D. 900 Globe's inviting location in sheltering hills beside a reliable stream led the wandering Hohokam people to dig a cluster of pit houses on a Pinal Creek overlook southeast of downtown. For about two centuries they thrived, then abandoned the site. In A.D. 1225, the Salado people built an adobe pueblo trading center atop the Hohokam site, housing as many as 400 people in over 200 rooms. Skilled farmers who made ingenious and extensive use of irrigation ditches, the Salado were also driven away by an extended dry period in the 15th century. The 700-year-old pueblo

Kiva interior, Besh-Ba-Gowah Archaeological Park

complex is the centerpiece of **Besh-Ba-Gowah Archaeological Park ★★** *(Jesse Hayes Rd. 520-425-0320. Adm. fee).* Here the desert ends and mountainous pine forest begins. (Bridging two rich plant zones, the location helped enrich the Salado diet.) Visitors to Besh-Ba-Gowah ("place of metal") may explore the pueblo on their own. Climb re-created old-style ladders to its upper levels and duck through a narrow, windowless central corridor to the pueblo's inner plaza. Inside, you'll find examples of the tools and pottery used here seven centuries ago. Many artifacts recovered at this site are exhibited in the nearby museum, which has the Southwest's most complete collection of Salado pottery—some of the most sophisticated graphic design found in Native American handicrafts.

Heading east, US 70 enters the 1.5-million-acre ❸ **San Carlos Apache Reservation** *(Tribal recreation and wildlife headquarters in Peridot 520-475-2343),* ancestral homeland of the legendary Geronimo, who led the Apache through a decade of sporadic resistance against Anglo-American encroachment. The road follows the Gila River Valley southeast past often striking landscapes of eroded basin and range. It then vaults the 5,000-foot hump of the Peloncillo Mountains to land in Duncan and pick up Ariz. 75 north.

Ariz. 75 leads to US 191 and **④** **Clifton,** center of another Arizona mining frenzy, this one for copper. (One turn-of-the-century claim paid its owner 3.5 million dollars a year.) By the 1880s downtown's Chase Creek Street was a rowdy boulevard of eateries and shops squeezed between saloons and bordellos. Some ruffians ended up in the town's **Old Jail** *(520-865-4146),* a cave at the base of the mountainside rising from South Coronado Boulevard. The narrow-gauge mining locomotive on display here once hauled copper ore from Metcalf to Clifton's smelter.

Continue north on US 191 and take a tour of the **Morenci Mine** *(520-865-4521 ext. 435. Mon.-Fri.),* the second largest open pit copper mine in the world. The original townsite was moved to make way for the expanding crater.

The scenic drive north through Arizona's central highlands and the **Apache-Sitgreaves National Forests** *(520-333-4301)* purportedly follows the route taken in 1540 by Francisco Vasquez de Coronado in his 1,300-man quest for the fabled Seven Cities of Cibola. In 60 miles the Coronado Trail passes through the entire range of life zones found between Mexico and Canada, climbing 5,000 feet from desert to alpine forest and meadows.

About 53 miles north of Clifton, there's an impressive cross-country view from the watchtower atop 8,786-foot **Rose Peak.** Look for signs indicating the Rose Peak Trail

Morenci open pit copper mine, near Clifton

parking area. The half-mile
path up is easy underfoot,
but the altitude might soon
have your heart beating fast.

Another 25 minutes
north, and you'll slip over
the edge of the thousand-
foot-high **Mogollon Rim.**
Two thousand feet high in
places, the escarpment is the
southernmost edge of the

Hannagan Meadow Lodge

Colorado Plateau—a tableland with rock layers up to 1.8
billion years old. Stop at 9,184-foot-high **Blue Vista** summit for truly spectacular views across the rumpled,
forested landscape of mountains and valleys.

Five miles north—still at 9,100 feet—you'll come to
❺ **Hannagan Meadow ★,** one of Arizona's most popular
camping spots. From late spring through autumn it's a
verdant and peaceful grassland bowl sprinkled with a profusion of wildflowers. Come winter, it's a busy jumping-off
point for cross-country skiers. There's a lovely log lodge
and store here, making the meadow a convenient stop.
Take a stroll out across the wild grass, breathe deeply,
and savor the mind-clearing combination of breezy stillness, crystalline air, and brilliant sunlight.

The next 23 miles take you along the eastern flank of
the White Mountains to 8,050-foot-high **Alpine** *(Chamber
of Commerce 520-339-4330)* in the so-called Arizona Alps.
The diminutive town, founded in 1879 by Mormons, is a
much used entry point and trailhead into the exceptionally
popular fishing, camping, and wildlife-viewing areas inside
the Apache-Sitgreaves National Forests.

Continuing north, you'll rise and fall through meadow
and forest country before landing in ❻ **Springerville**
(Chamber of Commerce 520-333-2123), where the Little
Colorado River winds across Round Valley at 7,000 feet.
Before his fateful career change, Billy (the Kid) Bonney
poked cows here. Blame his wild and abbreviated youth
on the corrupting influence of the murderous cattle
rustlers who controlled the surrounding *Valle Redondo*
until the turn of the century. Their days were barely over
when the first automobile (a Pathfinder convertible) to
cross the country chugged westbound through the cheer-
ing town in 1910. Downtown, you'll find the main Forest

Service office for the Apache-Sitgreaves *(520-333-4301).* On Main Street there's a heroic statue of a pioneer woman known as the **Madonna of the Trail,** symbolizing women who ventured west across 19th-century North America.

About 2 miles northwest of town on a site overlooking the Little Colorado River stands the 700-year-old Mogollon Indian pueblo at **Casa Malpais National Historic Landmark** ★ *(318 Main St. 520-333-5375. Fee for tour).* Casa Malpais ("house of badlands") is notable for its network of burial catacombs. Like Besh-Ba-Gowah, it was abandoned after about two centuries. The ruins, dating from A.D. 1200, are open only by guided tours leaving three times daily from the downtown museum, where a wealth of artifacts from the site is on display.

The 47-mile run to the junction with Ariz. 260 traverses some of the loneliest looking country on your trip. Early settlers liked it that way. By 1875 former Army scout Corydon Cooley and neighbor Marion Clark, who jointly owned a townsite, had gotten on each other's nerves and agreed that one of them had to move. Problem was, neither wanted to. They sat down for a game of poker. On the last hand, Clark warned Cooley that unless he could "show low," his two Apache wives would soon be packing his buckboard. Cooley drew a card. "Show low it is," said he, laying down the deuce of clubs and taking full ownership of **Show Low** *(Chamber of Commerce 520-537-2326).* As you roll along Deuce of Clubs Street, you'll see a town catering to fishing, hunting, and rodeo riding. Anglers come to fish **Fool Hollow Lake,** northwest of town, and **Show Low Lake,** which lies just south.

For more water, follow Ariz. 260 south and east to **❼ Pinetop-Lakeside** *(Chamber of Commerce 520-367-4290),* whose picture-postcard lakes and streams make it a popular summer resort destination.

After leaving the Mogollon Rim near Indian Pine, turn right onto Ariz. 73. This lovely route runs south along the White River's North Fork on the 1.6-million-acre **White Mountain Apache Reservation** *(Whiteriver Tribal Headquarters 520-338-4346; for permits call Game and Fish Dept. 520-338-4385).* Outdoor enthusiasts recommend the reservation's 26 lakes and 400 miles of fishing streams for camping and hiking in solitude.

In the late 1800s **Fort Apache** ★ was an important Army outpost and one of the most remote, strategically

Kinishba Ruins, near Whiteriver

positioned between Apache homelands to the south and
Navajo country to the north. About 4 miles south of
Whiteriver, Fort Apache preserves about 20 of the garri-
son's original buildings on the grounds of the Theodore
Roosevelt Indian School, where the **Apache Office of
Tourism** *(520-338-1230)* and the **White Mountain
Apache Cultural Center**★ *(520-338-4625. Adm. fee)* share
quarters. The cultural center's exhibits tell dramatic tales
of the rocky historical road the tribe traveled to this piece
of ground and offers insight into the lifestyles, arts and
crafts, customs, and spiritual outlook that distinguish
Apache from other Native American people.

About nine centuries ago, you would have found a
settlement of Mogollon people at the site 7 miles southwest of Whiteriver known as **Kinishba Ruins** *(520-338-
1230 for road conditions)*. This is one of the largest and most
complete Mogollon pueblos in Arizona, and well worth
visiting. About 2 miles west of the Fort Apache Junction
on Ariz. 73, watch for a sign directing you onto Reservation Road 42. Two miles down the dirt road are the
remains of what originally were three sandstone pueblos,
parts of which rise three stories, leading archaeologists to
estimate that as many as 2,000 people lived here in a
complex of about 400 rooms between A.D. 1100 and 1350.

Continue northwest on Ariz. 73 to US 60/Ariz. 77 near
Carizzo. Turn left and enjoy the piney vistas as you travel
southwest to **Salt River Canyon**★. In many ways this
5-mile-wide chasm is a miniature of the Grand Canyon.
Its plunging, steep-stepped cliff walls of limestone and

sedimentary rock, soaring spires, and lofty caprock mesas glow with the same rich dusky hues. Drive with caution on the multiple switchbacks leading down into the

Salt River, Salt River Canyon

canyon, and take advantage of the pullouts to stop and admire the vertical beauty. The perspective on the cliffs rising above you is especially dramatic. (Watch for a safe pull off to use as an extended stop.) Take your picnic basket with you to the riverside rest area and keep your eyes open for petroglyphs. At this point the Salt River is still free flowing; make use of the pedestrian bridge to experience its splendor. Keep in mind: To hike or drive off of US 60/Ariz. 77 on the Apache reservation, you will need to obtain a permit at the White Mountain Apache store near the rest area *(for information call 520-338-4385 or 520-475-2343)*.

Follow US 60/Ariz. 77 back to Globe and head west on US 70 about 5 miles to the junction with Ariz. 88. Take this northwest to ❽ **Tonto National Monument** ★ ★ *(520-467-2241. Lower Ruin open daily, Upper Ruin Nov.-April weekends only; adm. fee).* The cliff dwellings nestled under quartzite overhangs here were built sometime around A.D. 1100 by the Salado people, who grew corn, beans, squash, and cotton by irrigating the valley below. They thrived for some 300 years, then, like the Mogollon, vanished around 1450. If you can spare an hour, have a look at the Lower Ruin, one of the most accessible in the region. You'll need walking shoes for the half-mile paved trail to the 19-room masonry structure, as the path climbs about 350 vertical feet and is fairly steep. There's a bigger dwelling higher up—the impressive 40-room Upper Ruin—at the end of a rocky 1.5-mile trail. That's a three-hour round-trip, and you'll need reservations for the guided tour.

By now you've admired **Theodore Roosevelt Lake** glittering on the desert to the north. Ecological and historical exhibits at the new **Roosevelt Lake Visitor Center** *(520-467-3200)* tell the story of the 23-mile-long reservoir created by **Theodore Roosevelt Dam** (1.25 miles farther west), which backs up the flow of the Salt River. Starting in 1903, engineers began to fit the dam's hand-hewn limestone blocks together. By 1911 they'd piled them 280 feet high and 723 feet wide, which in those days qualified as the world's largest masonry dam. The 1,080-foot-long bridge across the gorge is America's longest two-lane, single-arch, steel span.

The next 32 miles take you along the scenic basin between the Mazatzal Mountains to the west and the Sierra Ancha to the east, through the dusty pioneer-era map dots of **Punkin Center** and **❾ Jakes Corner,** where ranch folk linger at roadside general stores to catch up on local gossip in this spread-out country.

When Ariz. 188 meets Ariz. 87, turn left (south) for a scenic 60-mile cruise to **❿ Tempe.** As you've roamed, you've probably wondered once or twice what it might be like to move here and live in this country, how your lifestyle might change. For insights into how newcomers from Spanish colonials to Sun City retirees have adapted to desert life, visit the **Arizona Historical Society Museum★** *(1300 N. College Ave. 602-929-0292)* in Papago Park, just east of the airport. (From Ariz. 87 turn right on McDowell Road and head west. Turn left onto 68th Street, which becomes College Avenue when you enter Tempe.) Exhibits and multimedia presentations span 1,100 years of Arizona history, from Hohokam pit-house villages to the air-conditioned Southwest suburbs of today. You might be surprised to see how the Valley of the Sun has profoundly reshaped the heritage, culture, and lifestyle of each successive wave of new arrivals. From the looks of things—not least of all the phenomenal growth continuing in the Phoenix area—the sum in human satisfaction is greater than the parts.

Hedgehog cactus in bloom, Salt River Canyon

Tucson-Organ Pipe Loop★

● **450 miles** ● **2½ to 3 days** ● **All year** ● **Good roads throughout**

Tucson's growth from a Tohono O'odham Indian settlement and Spanish colonial outpost informs the historical pageant celebrated by the city's wealth of museums and Southwestern architecture. But it is the Sonoran Desert's pervasive presence—the heat, aridity, beauty, and perfect stillness—that seems to affect visitors most. Desert museums and parks let you mingle with the Sonoran's famous saguaro legions and come eye to eye with its wildlife—creatures so elusive they make the coyote seem sociable. Kitt Peak astronomers direct your gaze to distant worlds while scientists at Biosphere 2 study ecosystems here on earth. The ruins of prehistoric farming cultures—and the lonely adobe outposts of European-American territorial entrepreneurs—testify that human endeavor in this region has always been an uncertain adventure, always hostage to the desert's implacable character.

❶ **Tucson★** *(Convention and Visitors Bureau 520-624-1817)* has long held a reputation as a health resort, its annual average of over 350 sunny days touted as a general palliative. To the ears of the Spanish, the Tohono O'odham words for "spring at the foot of a dark mountain," what they called their settlement here, sounded like *chuk shon*. Their adobe enclave, established in 1775, thus became El Presidio San Augustin del Tucson. Downtown, **El Presidio Park** embraces the site of the original settlement. The surrounding El Presidio District, bounded by Pennington, Franklin, Church, and Main Streets, is rich in architecture and easy to explore with the help of the free "Tucson Official Visitors Guide."

The **Pima County Courthouse** *(115 N. Church St. 520-740-3510. Open during business hours)* dates only from 1927 but is often cited as Arizona's prettiest example of modern Spanish colonial architecture. Inside, the building displays a portion of an adobe wall from the presidio. North across Alameda Street in the El Presidio District are several buildings listed in the National Register of Historic Places, including **La Casa Cordova★** *(175 N. Meyer Ave. 520-624-2333)*, an adobe residence built circa 1850. It houses the **Presidio History Room★,** filled with authentic Native American and Spanish colonial artifacts. Two blocks south on Alameda stands one of Tucson's oldest adobes, the

Sosa-Carillo-Frémont House Museum★ *(Tucson Convention Center Complex, 151 S. Granada. 520-622-0956. Wed.-Sat.),* furnished in the Mexican-American style of the 1880s.

Drive north on Granada Street as it merges with Main Street, turning right onto University Boulevard and continuing on to the **University of Arizona** *(520-621-5130)*. Park in the university

Apache woman and child at powwow near Tucson

lot, or take advantage of the free parking up the street at the **Arizona Historical Society Museum★** *(949 E. Second St. 520-628-5774)*. Exhibits here highlight the key influences in Arizona's past: Native American and Mexican cultures, European exploration, mining, and ranching. The "Mining Hall" exhibit includes a stamp mill and a re-created mining camp, including a very realistic "underground" mine tunnel.

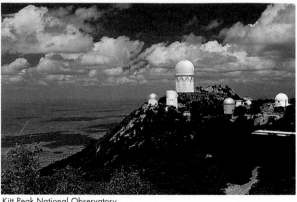

Kitt Peak National Observatory

Western Topper

The cowboy hat we know best—wide, curved brim, creased crown—actually came late to the Wild West. Until the 1880s, flat-brimmed, flat-topped pillbox planter's hats—usually tan, gray, or off-white—and bowlers like the one sported by bank robber Butch Cassidy, were common. Philadelphia hat-maker John B. Stetson made his first bid for the Western market in 1865, introducing the Boss of the Plains, an open-crown, wide-brim affair. Business boomed. Another Stetson best seller, the Carlsbad, was popular from 1920 to 1940. Its owners personalized theirs by creasing the crown and rolling the brim. Hat sizes grew ever larger, culminating in El Monster, which had an 8-inch brim and a 5-plus-inch crown. And, unlike the movies, hat colors varied; the good guy didn't always wear white.

Back on campus, the **Arizona State Museum** *(Park Ave. and University Blvd. 520-621-6302)* houses what many consider the finest collection of Southwestern American Indian art and artifacts anywhere. Nearby, the **Center for Creative Photography** ★★ *(Fine Arts Complex 520-621-7968. Closed Sat.)* archives work by over 1,800 photographers, including Louise Dahl-Wolfe, W. Eugene Smith, Edward Weston, and Ansel Adams. To arrange an hour-long personal viewing of work by almost any of the photographers in the center's collection, call in advance.

When you're ready to explore the Sonoran Desert, take Speedway Boulevard west to Gates Pass Road through Tucson Mountain Regional Park, then turn right onto Kinney Road to the **Arizona-Sonora Desert Museum** ★★ *(2021 N. Kinney Rd. 520-883-2702. Adm. fee)*. More zoo than museum, the 30-acre complex compresses the Sonoran Desert's 120,000-square-mile sprawl across southern Arizona and California and northern Mexico into a cluster of re-created habitats for over 300 native animals and some 1,300 plants. The Cactus Garden exhibits over 260 Sonoran Desert plant species, including 131 cactuses. To see animals, come early when temperatures are cooler.

Continue northwest on Kinney Road about a mile to the western district of **Saguaro National Park** ★ *(Red Hills Visitor Center 520-733-5158)*. The giant saguaro cactus *(Carnegiea gigantea)* is the Sonoran Desert's trademark and can grow more than 40 feet high (see sidebar page 112). Those with several large arms are usually over 150 years old. The 6-mile gravel Bajada Loop Drive winds through an extremely dense saguaro forest to the **Signal Hill Picnic Area.** Here rocks display Hohokam petroglyphs etched through the brown patina of iron-manganese oxide called desert varnish.

About 40 miles from Tucson on Ariz. 86, turn left onto Kitt Peak Road (Ariz. 386) and follow the winding route 12 miles to the **❷ Kitt Peak National Observatory** and the **National Solar Observatory** *(520-318-8726. Donations)*. With 22 specialized telescopes, this is the world's largest facility for stellar, solar, and planetary research. Astron- omers are sometimes available to answer questions, and guided tours are free. The views are spectacular, and there's a roadside picnic area about 1.4 miles from the summit. (The ancient Tohono O'odham considered the spire of nearby Baboquivari Peak the universe's center.)

Continue west to **Sells,** headquarters of the 2.3-million-acre **Tohono O'odham Reservation** *(520-383-2221)*, the state's second largest after the Navajo. The tribe, formerly known as Papago, revived their aboriginal name, which means "desert people." Tribal artisans sell their distinctive pottery and baskets here and throughout the reservation.

From **❸ Why**—formerly Y, named for the wishbone junction of highways here—head south into strikingly picturesque Sonoran Desert landscapes. If you can spare half a day and don't mind gravel roads, head south on

Multistemmed organ pipe, solitary saguaros, teddybear chollas, and yellow-flowered brittlebrushes

Casa Grande Ruins National Monument, near Coolidge

Ariz. 85 for 22 scenic miles to **Organ Pipe Cactus National Monument** ★ *(Visitor Center 520-387-6849. Adm. fee).* The night-blooming organ pipe cactuses are found mainly in Mexico, and this 517-square-mile desert garden includes the largest colony of these multi-armed expatriates north of the border. The 53-mile **Puerto Blanco Drive** leads to the spring-fed oasis of Quitobaquito; the 21-mile **Ajo Mountain Drive** wriggles up to lofty overlooks where 20-foot-tall organ pipe, resembling the hands of skeletons, grasp at the sky.

The appropriately named ❹ **Gila Bend** was formed in the mid-1880s where the Gila River takes a 90-degree turn. Exhibits at the **Gila Bend Museum** *(644 W. Pima St. 602-683-2002)* display artifacts from the region.

Continue eastbound on I-8, which merges with I-10. As you near Casa Grande, you'll see the 3,370-foot-high spike of eroded lava identifying ❺ **Picacho Peak State Park** *(520-466-3183. Adm. fee)*, site of Arizona's largest Civil War clash. In April 1862, 13 Union soldiers dispatched from California encountered 17 Confederate cavalrymen here. Two short trails lead to the summit, but the hand-over-hand ascent is recommended only for hikers in good shape and wearing leather gloves.

Backtrack northwest on I-10 to Ariz. 87/287. Near Coolidge, Ariz. 87 merges with Arizona Boulevard. Look for signs to **Casa Grande Ruins National Monument** ★

(520-723-3172. *Adm. fee*), the ruins of a Hohokam village dating from A.D. 1350. A four-story structure dominates the site; archaeologists believe it was used for religious ceremonies, astronomy, or food storage. The Hohokam once thrived in this region by irrigating the desert with river water diverted by a 600-mile canal network.

Return to Ariz. 87/287 and continue on Ariz. 287 east to the peaceful little town of Florence and ❻ **McFarland Historical State Park** (*Ruggles and Main Sts. 520-868-5216. Thurs.-Mon.; adm. fee*), named for mid-century political powerhouse Ernest W. McFarland, who served Arizona as U.S. senator, governor, and state supreme court justice. Legal tomes, lawyerly furnishings, and other memorabilia are displayed in the adobe Pinal County Courthouse.

Take Ariz. 79 southeast to Oracle Junction, turning left onto Ariz. 77 north toward Oracle and the Santa Catalina Mountains. Turn right at mile marker 96.5 and follow the road to ❼ **Biosphere 2** (*520-896-6200 or 800-828-2462. Adm. fee*). Here, under Columbia University's aegis, scientists work in a 3.15-acre laboratory encased in steel and glass, studying the effects of greenhouse gases on plants and, ultimately, human life. Modeled on Biosphere 1—the part of the planet Earth that sustains life—Biosphere 2 contains five distinct ecosystems: rain forest, savanna, ocean, marsh, and desert. Interpretive exhibits in the Visitor Center and a 0.75-mile guided walking tour emphasize the Earth and its environment.

Backtrack to Ariz. 79 and turn south on Ariz. 77 toward Tucson. You'll soon come to **Catalina State Park** (*520-628-5798*), a natural arboretum of desert plants and haven for over 150 bird species. Trails weave through its rugged scrub and cactus foothills, and you can camp overnight in their deep solitude.

Sabino Canyon shuttle bus

Once back in Tucson—particularly if you see a pretty sunset shaping up—drive to the top of **Sentinel Mountain** (*W on Congress St., then left at Sentinel Peak Rd.*) for a sweeping panorama of the far desert horizon.

Sabino Canyon ★

Tucsonites flock to **Sabino Canyon** (*N. Sabino Canyon Rd. 520-749-8700. Fee for shuttle bus*) the way folks in coastal cities head for the beach, and you should too. Once there, you'll leave your car and hop onto an open-air shuttle for a ride up past sheer cliff faces cut by the falling water of Sabino Creek, as it tumbles over boulders and waterfalls. The narrated tour takes about 45 minutes and stops at picnic spots, swimming holes, and trailheads. You can wander off into this unusually scenic corner of the Coronado National Forest—where the only evergreens are cactuses.

105

The Border Region ★★

● 475 miles ● 3 to 4 days ● All year (but call ahead for road conditions when weather is wet or snowy) ● Mostly paved roads; some side trips on gravel and graded dirt roads may be too steep or curvy for long RVs and car-trailer combinations.

106

Statue under repair,
Mission San Xavier del Bac

This drive through Arizona's historical heartland above the Mexican border spans the centuries that created the Southwest's distinctive culture. A memorial to Coronado overlooks the place where Spanish conquistadores first marched into what would become the United States, and missions commemorate the Spanish colonial vision. Ageless wildlife havens are preserved throughout the region, where bloody Indian wars pitted the U.S. Army against the Apache. And town-size relics of Arizona's turbulent boom-bust mining era remain where gunfighters finally came to extinction, in the last dangerous corner of the American Wild West.

Begin the drive along I-19 south of Tucson, where **❶ Mission San Xavier del Bac★★** *(1950 San Xavier Rd. 520-294-2624. Mass celebrated daily)* was founded in 1700. The present Spanish baroque church, completed in 1797, is called the White Dove of the Desert for the luminosity of its pale stucco walls. The elaborately carved stone portal hints at the intricate carvings and frescoes within.

Continue south on I-19 to a world as far removed from San Xavier as any could be. Take the Duval Mine Road exit and head west, watching for signs to the **Titan Missile Museum** *(1580 W. Duval Mine Rd. 520-791-2929. Daily Nov.- Apr., Wed.-Sun. May-Oct.),* a relic of America's Cold War-era doomsday machine. Between 1982 and 1987, the U.S. Air Force decommissioned its arsenal of Titan II intercontinental ballistic missiles— ten-story-high rockets tipped with nuclear warheads over 200 times more powerful than the bomb that devastated Hiroshima. The disarmed Titan II displayed here in its original launching silo is the only one still in existence.

Springtime festival, Mission San Xavier del Bac

After your brush with Armageddon, you may wish to calm yourself with a side trip to the **Madera Canyon Recreation Area** *(520-670-5464)* in the Coronado National Forest's Santa Rita Mountains. Take the White House Canyon Road off I-19 and head southeast. Birders have identified nearly 400 migratory species here.

Originally a Pima farming hamlet, now an outpost of bohemia, **Tubac★** is generally regarded as Arizona's first European settlement, founded in 1726 with the construction of a Jesuit church. The spiky Santa Rita Mountains make such a gorgeous backdrop, it is no wonder the town's one thousand souls include many artists and artisans. Their work supplies the village's many galleries and shops.

In 1859 Arizona's first newspaper, *The Weekly Arizonian,* was lifted off a handpress here, and by the following year the town was the largest in the territory. Relics of the bygone days are preserved in the 10-acre **Tubac Presidio State Historic Park ★** *(Presidio Dr. 520-398-2252. Adm. fee)* at the town's center. The 1885 schoolhouse survives, along with old ruins built atop what remains of the original Spanish fort. The museum features an excavated foundation cross section from the captain's house, revealing layers of historical accretion—Pima potsherds, Spanish glassware, and rusty Anglo-American iron.

Tubac shopping district

Local myth holds that padres who abandoned Mission San José de Tumacacori in 1848 left behind a buried cache of gold and silver. For the next half-century fortune seekers regularly dug around the ruins preserved at ❷ **Tumacacori National Historical Park** ★ ★ *(Off I-19. 520-398-2341. Adm. fee).* The mission was founded in 1691, but Apache attacks, a brutal winter, and Mexico's refusal of funds prevented the completion of the second, more elaborate church. Sanctuary ruins and a cemetery remain from the first church. The Visitor Center's patio garden is landscaped with plants cultivated during the mission era.

Friendly ❸ **Nogales** *(520-287-3685)* is best known as a crossing point into Mexico and the casual markets of its larger Mexican sister city in Sonora, well stocked with leather goods, baskets, and pottery. American Nogales's old City Hall now houses the **Pimeria Alta Historical Society Museum** *(136 N. Grand Ave. 520-287-4621. Tues.-Sat.),* an archive of old books, photographs, maps, journals, and exhibits documenting the last ten centuries of life in

108

Mission San José de Tumacacori, Tumacacori National Historical Park

southern Arizona and northern Mexico. The museum also offers information on self-guided walking tours.

If you'd like to sleep under the stars at 4,000 feet, note your odometer as you leave Nogales and, after about 12 miles, look left for the turnoff to **Patagonia Lake State Park ★** *(520-287-6965)*. You'll find campsites along a pretty 265-acre lake fringed with mesquite and shade trees. A footbridge arcs gracefully over an arm of the lake, and a trail wanders off into the desert.

Bird-watchers and serenity seekers flock to the Nature Conservancy's **Patagonia-Sonoita Creek Preserve** *(520-394-2400. Wed.-Sun., nature walks Sat. a.m.; donations)*. The 350-acre haven of cottonwood and willow includes a 1.5-mile stretch of creekside habitat supporting 275 bird species and creatures like bobcats, coatis, javelinas, and white-tailed deer. You can't camp or picnic here— extended human presence would affect the preserve's ecological balance—but visitors are welcome. Turn left off Ariz. 82 onto Fourth Avenue and follow it to its end, then go left on the well-maintained dirt road.

From here, Ariz. 82 travels northeast across some of the Southwest's finest grazing land, often compared to the Argentine pampas. ❹ **Patagonia,** like Tubac, is a little tree-lined hamlet with a contingent of creative people who value its mix of rural and urban; art galleries and rustic country stores, bookstores and saddle shops, friendly saloons and at least one espresso bar await.

Hummingbird, Patagonia Hills

Set on breezy desert grassland at 4,623 feet, **Sierra Vista** *(520-458-6940 or 800-288-3861)* plays host to the U.S. Army's **Fort Huachuca ★** *(520-538-7111. Map and visitor's pass at main gate),* founded in 1877 to protect settlers from rebellious Chiricahua Apache led by Cochise and Geronimo. Headquarters of the Army's Intelligence Center, the fort preserves an Old Post area—a national historic landmark with vintage buildings from the territorial era. The mounted B Troop cavalry quartered here dons frontier-era uniforms and performs throughout the Southwest.

As many as 12 of Arizona's 15 species of hummingbirds migrate through this region every year between April and August. If you're here then, stop at the Nature Conservancy's 300-acre **Ramsey Canyon Preserve** *(27 Ramsey Canyon Rd. 520-378-2785. Call ahead for parking reservations; donations),* and view one of the most diverse seasonal gatherings of these blurry-winged buzz-bombs anywhere in North America. They're joined by more than 135 other varieties of feathered nomads. Why? A fast-flowing creek waters the steep-walled canyon, creating a desert oasis also supporting white-tailed deer and coatis. Camping, picnicking, pets, and rigs longer than 18 feet are forbidden. If you still qualify, go south 6 miles from Sierra Vista on Ariz. 92, turning right (west) onto Ramsey Canyon Road.

The wars between aboriginal North Americans and European newcomers had their symbolic beginning in 1540 about 22 miles south of Sierra Vista. From this site Spanish adventurer Francisco Vasquez de Coronado led 336 caballeros and foot soldiers, several hundred hired Mexican-Indian helpers, 1,500 stock animals, and four priests north via the San Pedro River Valley on a treasure-hunting "expedition of conquest" across what is today the U.S.-Mexico border. The quest brought north the mixing of Mexican, Spanish, and Native American blood and heritage into a cultural amalgam, giving the American Southwest its unique character. This epochal event is the theme of the little museum at the lofty ❺ **Coronado National Memorial** ★ *(4101 E. Montezuma Canyon Rd. 520-366-5515. Adm. fee),* a Park Service outpost at 5,280 feet. To get there, take Ariz. 92 south to Coronado Road. Turn right (south) and follow it 2 miles, turning right again on Montezuma Canyon Road. Displays of re-created Spanish armor and weaponry contrast with depictions of agrarian pueblo life. The 4,750-acre memorial is a day-use area with a network of hiking trails. A new hike will lead 1.5 miles south, to the boundary with Mexico.

Had Coronado followed your route east, his vision of riches might have been realized in the silver country surrounding ❻ **Tombstone** ★★ *(Visitor Center, Fourth and Allen Sts. 520-457-3929),* the capital of Arizona's Wild West country and the quintessential example of a two-fisted,

Cowboys and dance hall girls, Tombstone

110

hard-drinking, trigger-happy boomtown. It acquired its forbidding moniker when prospector Ed Schieffelin struck a rich vein of silver in 1877, after skeptics warned that all he'd find in these rocky hills was his tombstone. The ensuing silver rush brought opportunity seekers of every moral persuasion, and the town remade itself to profit from their notions of fun. By the mid 1880s, the city was the most populous between St. Louis and San Francisco, and its mines had shipped 25 million dollars in silver—a colossal sum in an era of nickel shots of red-eye.

As you approach Tombstone, turn right onto Ariz. 80, which sneaks into town under the alias of Fremont Street. There's so much overcommercialized history here that you'll do well to start with a no-nonsense overview at **Tombstone Courthouse State Historic Park ★** *(219 E. Toughnut St. 520-457-3311. Adm. fee).* Turn left onto Third Street and follow it two blocks south to Toughnut Street. The splendid two-story, stone-and-brick building cost about $50,000 in 1882. Inside are exhibits on local mining and history, and the building's courtroom has been re-created. The park outside is a pleasant place to picnic away from the bustle of downtown.

Walk north to **Allen Street,** where Tombstone's historical fervor reaches critical mass in a chockablock squeeze of souvenir shops, old-style stores, piano saloons, quasi-historical attractions, and amusing eateries. Between Third and Fourth Streets you'll find the **OK Corral** *(520-457-3456. Adm. fee).* Though famous, the old horse pen is not quite the site of the 1881 shoot-out that pitted Wyatt Earp, two siblings, and their tubercular ally Doc Holliday against the Clanton and McLaury brothers. (The battle occurred nearby.) Often portrayed as a clash of personalities, the feud also arose from business rivalries.

An example of Tombstone's odd 19th-century mix of roughness and refinement is the **Bird Cage Theater** *(Sixth and Allen Sts. 520-457-3421. Adm. fee).* Originally a music hall and sin den, it now displays an engaging hodge-podge of antiques and curios from Tombstone's past. Caruso sang opera here, and superstars Sarah Bernhardt and Lillian Russell reduced roughneck audiences to tears. The establishment got its name from what then passed for creative marketing: Professional ladies were hoisted to the ceiling in cages, allowing prospective patrons to make considered choices.

Hidden Treasures

Ever since Coronado searched for the Seven Cities of Gold, people have believed in legends of hidden treasure in the southwest. Author J. Frank Dobie collected the stories in his book, *Coronado's Children.* In one tale the shifting sands of Arizona's desert reveal millions of gold nuggets to a Mexican shepherd girl. Another recounts how the whereabouts of a massive vein of pure gold in the New Mexico mountains is lost with the death of its discoverer. Greed and betrayal cause death and the lost wealth of a fabulous lode west of Tombstone. The stories share similarities: The original discoverer, unable to trace his path back to the find, goes mad or dies of disappointment; his only confidant vanishes; the only map is lost or a key piece is missing. Not one of these tales has led to riches, but the legends persist. Why? According to Dobie, the imagination abhors failure.

111

Saguaro at sunset

Saguaro National Park ★

Between Tucson and Colossal Cave, at the base of the Rincon Mountains, stands the eastern district of **Saguaro National Park** *(520-733-5153. Adm. fee).* Pick up driving and hiking guides at the Visitor Center, then travel 8-mile Cactus Forest Drive through old forests of massive saguaro, trademark of the Sonoran Desert. *Carnegiea gigantea* reach heights of 50 feet, sprouting arms only after about 75 years. The ones waving at you with several arms were already prickly little tykes well before the California gold rush. The short Desert Ecology Trail is designed to illustrate the role of water in arid environments, but is more likely to impress you with the powerful presence of the Sonoran Desert's perfect stillness.

112

Tuberculosis, mining mishaps, and hard living claimed more victims here than did the Colt .44, but in any case the deceased were usually trundled off to **Boot Hill Graveyard** *(520-457-9344. Adm. fee).* The two McLaury brothers and a Clanton are buried here—they lost the shoot-out—along with some 250 others, and perhaps 500 more without markers. Take Fremont Street to Tombstone's northwest fringe, where the sad-looking burial ground rises near the roadside.

Tombstone's silver veins petered out in the 1880s after glutted international markets depressed prices, and flooding mines made the silver inaccessible. But prosperity lasted longer in nearby **Bisbee★★** *(Visitor Center, 7 Main St. 520-432-5421),* which adjoins one of the richest copper lodes ever found in the United States. Renovated buildings in Bisbee's historic district still radiate success. Visitor Center brochures map out self-guided walking tours, including handsome Victorian neighborhoods on the mountainsides above. The last local mine closed in 1975, five years short of Bisbee's centennial, and the town's 6,500 residents still include a lot of retired miners. Its scenic setting, appealing architecture, relaxed civility, and good shops and restaurants account for a sizable contingent of urban émigrés and artists.

The **Copper Queen Hotel ★** *(11 Howell Ave. 520-432-2216),* built in 1902, is a survivor of early-century days, when Bisbee's population reached 25,000. The Queen is Arizona's oldest operating hotel, with a friendly restaurant, old-fashioned saloon, and outdoor balcony offering pleasant places to linger. Behind the hotel you'll find the **Bisbee Mining and Historical Museum** *(5 Copper Queen Plaza. 520-432-7071. Adm. fee)* in the century-old former headquarters of a company that ran most local mines. The museum's archive of 8,000 artifacts and 12,000 photographs document Bisbee's youth.

To see firsthand how Bisbee once earned a living (if you aren't claustrophobic), take the hour-long guided tour of the **Copper Queen Mine** *(118 Arizona St. 520-432-2071. Adm. fee),* across Ariz. 80 from the Brewery Gulch interchange. You'll ride a narrow-gauge ore train straight into a mountain in the company of veteran miner-guides. The tunnels are perfectly safe, but damp, drippy, and a chilly 47°F. Visitors are issued a yellow slicker, hard hat, and miner's lamp, but be sure to wear something warm.

Most of the ore shipped from Bisbee was smelted in
❼ Douglas, now a manufacturing center. The 1907
Gadsden Hotel ★ *(1046 G Ave. 520-364-4481)* features an
opulent lobby with a vaulted ceiling atop huge faux marble pillars with gold-leaf-covered capitals, stained-glass

Gadsden Hotel lobby, Douglas

skylights, a Tiffany window, and a white marble staircase
that begs for Fred Astaire to dance up and down it.

For a realistic sense of what it was like to ranch and
raise a family around here in the twilight of the Old West,
drive 16 miles out to **San Bernardino Ranch National
Historical Landmark ★** *(520-558-2474. Wed.-Sun.; adm.
fee).* Take 15th Street east from Douglas—it becomes
Geronimo Trail—to the home of cattleman John Slaughter
(1841-1922), a Texas Ranger who served as Cochise
County sheriff. You're free to tour the restored ranch on
your own and inspect the commissary, cook's quarters,
granary, icehouse, and other buildings required for self-sufficiency back then. The graded road to the ranch voyages across a rolling sea of scrub and grassland, evoking
the isolation of old-time Arizona rural life.

A 16-mile round-trip scenic drive winds through what
the Chiricahua Apache called the Land of the Standing-up
Rocks at **❽ Chiricahua National Monument ★**

(520-824-3560. Adm. fee). Some 20 miles of hiking trails wind through the monument's 12,000-acres, past erosion-sculptured balanced rock formations and towering columns to bracing mile-high views. This mountainous region has unusually wet summers (with thunderstorms almost daily) and a peculiar hybrid season in April and May, when the oak trees exhibit autumn colors as they finally decide to drop their leaves.

Chiricahua National Monument, with Cochise Head in distance

About 5 miles up Ariz. 186, look for signs indicating the turnoff onto Apache Pass Road, a graded dirt road that leads to **Fort Bowie National Historic Site** ★ *(520-847-2500).* The outpost, a relic of the U.S. Army's campaign against the Apache, was built in 1862 to protect the water spring for Union troops traveling east. Abandoned in 1894, the fort was scavenged by locals who left only the heavy stone foundations and adobe walls visible today. You must leave your car at a parking area and walk uphill 1.5 miles, winding past the old Butterfield Overland Stage station and the post cemetery to the fort's skeletal remains.

There's plenty doing in **❾ Willcox,** a picturesque little town that once proclaimed itself the Cattle Capital of America and still hosts Arizona's biggest livestock auction. If you really know your country and western music, it will mean something that Willcox is the hometown of Rex Allen, a singing cowpoke who starred in B pictures of the 1950s, including the appropriately titled *Arizona Cowboy.* The **Rex Allen Arizona Cowboy Museum** *(155 N. Railroad Ave. 520-384-4583. Adm. fee)* chronicles his durable career as well as honoring regional cowboys and cattle-industry figures.

You can't roam southeastern Arizona without gaining

an appreciation of Apache leader Cochise, a brilliant tactician who led the Chiricahua Apache into an unusually rugged region of the Dragoon Mountains in the 1860s. This wilderness of granite domes and sheer cliffs served as a nearly impregnable redoubt, known today as the ⑩ **Cochise Stronghold**★ *(520-826-3593. Adm. fee).* Here in 1872 Cochise negotiated a peace that held for nearly a decade until Geronimo's uprising. Near Sunsites, look for Forest Service signs indicating the turnoff onto Ironwood Road. At the Stronghold, an arched bridge over a creek begins a half-mile nature trail. There is also a historical loop trail with a dozen stops displaying informative signs about Cochise and the settlers, miners, and military who took part in his 11-year war against white settlement.

One of the world's preeminent collections of prehistoric and historic Native American artifacts is on display in **Dragoon** at the **Amerind Foundation Museum**★★ *(Dragoon Rd. 520-586-3666. June-Aug. Wed.-Sun., daily Sept.-May; adm. fee).* Here you'll find lovely Spanish colonial-style buildings filled with such treasures as old Apache spirit headdresses and baskets, ancient pottery, rare Navajo weavings, and Plains Indian beadwork and clothing. Self-trained archaeologist and art collector William Fulton established the foundation in 1937 to further understanding of Native American cultures, fashioning its name from "American" and "Indian." The shaded picnic area outside is a lovely place to savor the serenity of the surrounding country.

Autumn along Cave Creek, Coronado N.F.

Southern Pacific Railroad tracks parallel your route west. Legends abound from the 1880s of trains waylaid at nearby Pantano and robbed by four armed masked bandits who escaped a sheriff's posse by hiding in ⑪ **Colossal Cave** *(520-647-7275. Adm. fee).* The dry limestone cavern is among the largest in the United States, and its labyrinth of connecting rooms holds evidence of prehistoric Indian occupation. A guided walking tour leads through well-lit passages to lofty chambers columned with rising stalagmites and hanging stalactites. Exit off I-10 to the sleepy cow town of Vail, cross the tracks, and follow the road 5 miles into pretty Posta Quemada Canyon. Signs point to parking.

● **510 miles** ● **2 to 3 days** ● **All year, but fall and winter are best.**

116

Strings of chiles, called ristras, in Hatch

Railroads brought prosperity to southern New Mexico, whose old towns recall earlier times. The Mimbres once roamed this region, leaving few traces save the exquisite pottery that captivates museum visitors today. Mogollon families dwelled in the cliffs of what is now Gila National Forest. Here, too, linger the ghosts of 19th-century mining towns. To the east, where soldiers once rode to battle against rebellious tribes and Mexican invaders, Hatch reigns as the capital of New Mexico's chile country.

Travelers on the Camino Real trade route from Mexico passed through the Mesilla Valley as early as the 1600s. Crosses left in memory of the dead led locals to regard the place as La Placita de las Cruces. It took the arrival of railroad prosperity in 1881 to spur the growth of ❶ **Las Cruces** *(Visitors Bureau 505-524-8521 or 800-FIESTAS).*

The original townsite, laid out in 1849, is now part of the **Mesquite Historical District** *(E of Main St. between Picacho and Lohman),* an adobe neighborhood painted chalky hues of pink, blue, and green. In the 1800s addresses near the railroad station in the **Alameda–Depot Historical District** *(W of Main St. between Picacho and Amador)* were the most desirable. Its adobe buildings with Victorian trim were built by those whose fortunes came with the railroad.

The Eastern-bred Quaker who founded Las Cruces College in 1887 kept a black book identifying students caught in such sins as "smoking in the horse sheds" and "ball bouncing."

Shaded portal, Mesilla plaza

Hiram Hadley's school survived to become **New Mexico State University (NMSU).** The **NMSU Museum** *(University Ave. and Solano Dr. 505-646-3739. Closed Sat. and Mon.; donations)* has changing exhibitions on the history and culture of southern New Mexico and northern Mexico.

Until the railroad reached Las Cruces, adjoining **Mesilla** was the valley's social center. Many original buildings survive in the historic district around the old plaza, now filled with interesting shops and restaurants. Take Avenida de Mesilla west from downtown Las Cruces.

❷ **Deming** *(Chamber of Commerce 505-546-2674 or 800-848-4955)* grew up in 1881, when the last spike of the second coast-to-coast railroad was driven here. Set beside rugged mountains and fields of grain and cotton, its wide streets, husky brick and stone buildings, and capacious Victorians reflect the town's success as a cattle-shipping center. A walk along the redbrick **Silver Avenue Historic District** passes the old armory, now the **Deming Luna Mimbres Museum★** *(301 S. Silver St. 505-546-2382)*. Inside, 600 antique dolls roll glass eyes in surprised porcelain faces. If you haven't seen Mimbres pottery—prized by collectors as among the most elegant of any Southwest tribe's—those here are a good introduction.

In 1916 Mexican revolutionary Pancho Villa and 500 horsemen entered the country south of here to retaliate against American support of the Mexican government he wanted to overthrow. The raid left 18 Americans dead and sent General John Pershing 500 miles into Mexico after Villa's head. Villa escaped, and the misadventure boosted his folk hero status. Ironically, the controversial rebel is remembered at **Pancho Villa State Park** *(505-531-2711. Museum open on request; adm. fee)* in the little border town he raided, ❸ **Columbus.** The park holds what's left of the

New Mexico Chile

There are over 150 varieties of genus *Capsicum*—better known as chile. Most of the U.S. harvest comes from New Mexico. The burning sensation chiles give your tongue, called "heat," is a result of a chemical that stimulates the brain to produce endorphins, proteins responsible for the so-called runner's high and, among other things, a heightened sense of taste. Generally, the smaller the chile, the more heat it packs. One antidote is dairy products. Bread helps, water offers temporary relief, but alcoholic drinks only increase the heat. In New Mexican restaurants, the question "red or green?" asks you to choose between sauces and salsas made with young, green chiles, or ripe red ones. If you're wondering which is hotter, ask.

'13th U.S. Cavalry's Camp Furlong, target of Villa's wrath. Over 500 varieties of cactus grow here in a desert botanical garden. Local memorabilia is exhibited at the **Columbus Historical Society Museum** *(505-531-2620. Donations)* in the restored Southern Pacific Depot across the street.

Luckily, Villa's irregulars didn't know about nearby **Rock Hound State Park** *(505-546-6182. Adm. fee),* or they might have ridden north to fill their saddlebags with geodes, quartzes, opals, perlites, pitchstone, and agates. The park encourages visitors to collect the semiprecious stones, setting the limit at a pocket-busting 15 pounds. Exhibits show you what to look for outside. If you don't strike it semi-rich, trails across the landscape of cactuses, dry washes, and rock canyons below the Little Florida Mountains still deliver priceless beauty.

Like Las Cruces, ❹ **Lordsburg** *(Visitor Center 505-542-9864)* lagged behind a neighboring community until becoming a railhead while the other, a boomtown of 3,000, went bust. Its abandoned buildings occupy the privately owned **Shakespeare Ghost Town** *(505-542-9034. Guided tours second and fourth weekends of month; adm. fee).* A silver-mining mogul enamored of the immortal bard opened the Shakespeare Mine here, renamed the town, called its main drag Avon Avenue, and built the Stratford Hotel on it.

Mining and ranching built nearby ❺ **Silver City** *(Chamber of Commerce 505-538-3785 or 800-548-9378).* Its huge pit mines still produce copper, but the piney town is now primarily a mountain-country retreat. An old mansard-roofed Victorian houses the **Silver City Museum** *(312 W. Broadway. 505-538-5921. Tues.-Sun.),* brimming with mining paraphernalia, old-time furnishings and photographs, and Native American artifacts. The finest collection of Mimbres pottery in America is on display at the **Western New Mexico University Museum★★** *(505-*

Agave in bloom, Rock Hound State Park

538-6386), whose galleries also exhibit Hispanic folk art.

Although the Apache attempted to chase the miners out of **Pinos Altos** in 1861, many who stayed were successful in their search for gold. Presumably they enjoyed time in the **Buckhorn Saloon** *(505-538-9911)*, where you can still sidle up to the bar for a drink or enjoy a meal in the dining room. Signs guide you to the most interesting old buildings, including a schoolhouse, miners' shacks, and pioneer log cabins. Despite the town's rowdy youth, carved old-time monuments on Boot Hill exhibit prim Victorian motifs.

Shakespeare Ghost Town, near Lordsburg

Archaeologists believe the rock houses at **Gila Cliff Dwellings National Monument** ★★ *(N. Mex. 15. 505-536-9461)* sheltered up to 40 Mogollon people at any given time over a 25-year period, some seven centuries ago. You'll need sturdy walking shoes and about an hour to negotiate the 1-mile, self-guiding loop trail to a group of six caves, five of which contain a cluster of rooms ingeniously designed for maximum security.

To the south, erosion sculptured volcanic tuff into spires reaching 50 feet at **❻ City of Rocks State Park** *(N. Mex. 61. 505-536-2800. Adm. fee)*. They poke up from the desert like broken teeth; some see similarities to Stonehenge.

Head east into the Rio Grande Valley, which grows most of New Mexico's chile, and **❼ Hatch** *(505-267-5216)*, self-proclaimed Chile Capital of the World. The late-summer harvest brings thousands to town, where the many chile-oriented eateries here will amaze you with their variety of offerings. Douglas MacArthur liked to say that he learned to ride and shoot before he learned to read and write. No wonder: His father commanded the adobe Army post at what's now **Fort Selden State Monument** ★ *(I-25 and Fort Selden Rd. 505-526-8911)*, established in 1865 to protect Mesilla Valley settlers from hostile tribes. There's not much left, but photographs along a self-guided trail show how the fort looked during its active years. The museum has interpretive displays, and rangers in period uniforms demonstrate old-time soldierly skills. By 1891 the valley was peaceful, Fort Selden decommissioned, and the 11-year-old future general and his family moved to another post.

● 565 miles ● 3 to 4 days ● All year, but especially good in spring, when the desert blooms, and fall.

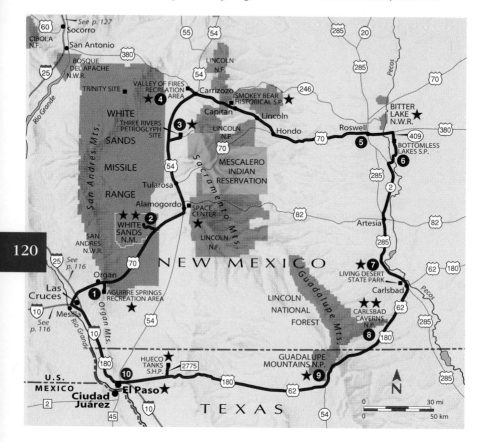

120

In southern New Mexico, history rivals natural beauty at such places as White Sands, where the first atomic bomb was detonated, and at Alamogordo, transformed into the country's rocket capital by America's first steps toward space. The region's last volcanic eruptions gave the Valley of Fires its name, near where Mescalero Apache chipped symbols into rock, proclaiming this territory theirs. Fires in Lincoln National Forest orphaned the cub who became Smokey Bear, while Lincoln's historical district preserves the epicenter of the Lincoln County Wars, a famed cowboy feud involving Billy the Kid. Underground erosion hollowed out the ancient ocean reef shaping the Guadalupe Mountains, leaving labyrinthine Carlsbad Caverns. The drive covers all this, before dipping into

Texas and El Paso, where the border between the United States and Mexico seems nearly erased.

Geologists tell you the Organ Mountains east of Las Cruces (see page 116) are 32 million-year-old Tertiary granite eroding along vertical joints. Locals just say they're pretty, especially when sunsets make them blush. East of 5,719-foot San Agustin Pass, you can picnic among their spires in **❶ Aguirre Springs Recreation Area★** *(505-525-4300. Adm. fee).* The 5.5-mile entrance road slaloms past granite pillars and a rock garden with agave and cactus to the high desert oasis.

West of US 70, what looks like a snow white sea with 60-foot waves is **❷ White Sands National Monument★★** *(505-479-6124. Adm. fee).* The world's largest gypsum dune system (about 300 square miles) results from wind blowing the crystals from the dry bed of nearby Lake Lucero, as it evaporates after filling with gypsum-rich mountain runoff. The 16-mile Dunes Drive has pullouts where you can stop to walk out into the wind-rippled wilderness.

White Sands National Monument

On occasion, the **White Sands Missile Range** *(505-678-1134)* will close the dunes and US 70 for two hours during tests. Here at 5:30 a.m. on July 16, 1945, Los Alamos scientists ushered in the atomic age by detonating a plutonium bomb. A stone obelisk marks the Trinity Site, still used by the military. The filled-in crater is off-limits, except on the first Saturdays of April and October.

Native agave

On that epochal morning, folks 55 miles away in **Alamogordo** *(Chamber of Commerce 505-437-6120)* awoke to a prolonged rumble and an eerie light in the northwest sky. The Army said a munitions bunker had exploded, but the lifting of wartime secrecy soon linked this little railroad town by the Sacramento Mountains with the bomb. After the war, rocket research took precedence at White Sands. Alamogordo's **Space Center**★ *(Scenic Dr. and Indian Wells Rd. 505-437-2840 or 800-545-4021. Adm. fee)* documents the adventure, which began with launches of captured German missiles. A wide-screen theater features planetarium displays, and walk-in exhibits simulate lunar and Martian landscapes and a space station interior. Early-generation rockets are displayed outdoors.

In the 1870s local cowhand Billy (the Kid) Bonney loaded stolen cattle at the Three Rivers railroad crossing. The old ranch road running east leads to over 500 prehistoric images chipped into rocks at the ❸ **Three Rivers Petroglyph Site**★ *(505-525-4300)*. A mile-long trail winds among the thousand-year-old symbols to partially reconstructed pueblos and pit houses.

About 1,500 years ago, just west of Carrizozo, searing volcanic lava from the vicinity of Little Black Peak crept across what became a "valley of fires." The flow solidified into a 4- to 5-mile-wide, 44-mile-long scar, one of the youngest lava deposits in the lower 48 states. A portion lies inside the ❹ **Valley of Fires Recreation Area**★ *(N. Mex. 380. 505-648-2241. Adm. fee)*, where a walking trail negotiates the jagged malpais, or badlands.

Smokey Bear existed only on paper until May 1950, when firefighters in the Lincoln National Forest found a badly burned cub clinging to a scorched tree. The patched-up orphan was soon on a plane to Washington, D.C.'s National Zoo, drafted into a 25-year tour of duty as the Forest Service mascot. The first Smokey is buried in **Capitan** *(Chamber of Commerce 505-354-2273)*, and his life and message are the theme of the town's **Smokey Bear Historical State Park** ★ *(505-354-2748)*. It's a nice picnic spot, with a short trail through gardens re-creating New Mexico's half-dozen biological life zones.

From 1878 to 1881, Lincoln County was New Mexico's least hospitable life zone. Here a feud between thugs monopolizing the region's lucrative beef industry and gun-toting rivals known as the Regulators claimed many lives before ending in a five-day battle. The Regulators enlisted Billy the Kid, fuzzycheeked at 18 but already wanted for murder in Arizona. The Lincoln County Wars are reenacted in **Lincoln** each August at the **Lincoln State Monument** ★ *(505-653-4372 or 653-4025. Adm. fee)*,

Southwestern Deserts

Four major desert systems combine to create the desert Southwest. Southwestern Arizona shares the cactus-populated Sonoran Desert with southeastern California and the Mexican states of Sonora and Baja California; the barren Mojave sprawls from southern Nevada and southern California into northwestern Arizona; southern New Mexico and west Texas share the scrubby Chihuahuan Desert with northern Mexico; and Utah's sagebrushy Great Basin Desert claims much of Nevada, overlapping eastern California, southeastern Oregon, and southern Idaho.

122

where many buildings figuring in the conflict are preserved. The museum occupies the courthouse and jail from which Billy, detained for the murder of Lincoln's sheriff, escaped by shooting two deputies. (He said he only felt bad about killing the one he liked.) Exhibits and living history guides sort out the bad guys from the not-quite-as-bad, and explain the deadly horse opera's convoluted plot.

A professional gambler turned hotel and store keeper founded **5 Roswell** *(Chamber of Commerce 505-623-5695)* to serve Texas cattlemen driving herds up the Pecos River Valley for sale to military posts. In 1912 a beef baron completed the mansion now housing the **Chaves County Historical Museum** *(200 N. Lea Ave. 505-622-8333. Fri.-Sun.; adm. fee).* Pick up the museum's map of the **Roswell Historic District ★,** which centers around Main and Second Streets and includes most of the architectural styles of the Old West. Turn south from Second onto Garden or Elm Street to enter a second picturesque district of old adobes.

Renowned regional art distinguishes the **Roswell Museum and Art Center ★ ★** *(100 W. 11th St. 505-624-6744),* which exhibits work by Georgia O'Keeffe, Marsden Hartley, John Marin, and John Sloan, among others. For something totally different, visit the museum's Goddard Wing and its reproduction of the workshop of liquid-fuel

Kit fox, Living Desert State Park

123

Big Room, Carlsbad Caverns National Park

El Capitan, view from Guadalupe Peak with Delaware Mountains in background

rocket pioneer Robert Goddard, who tested prototypes in Roswell from 1930 to 1941.

A seeming paradox in the desert Southwest are the seasonal populations of migratory waterfowl that use its wetlands for winter havens. The 24,000-acre **Bitter Lake National Wildlife Refuge★** *(505-622-6755)* hosts 300 species, including the sandhill crane. From October through February, sandhills step daintily into the lake to avoid the bobcats, foxes, and coyotes menacing the shore. Use the refuge's tour guide leaflet to follow the South Unit's 8-mile gravel loop trail.

There's a grain of truth in the myth that the ponds of **❻ Bottomless Lakes State Park** *(Visitor Center 505-624-6058. Adm. fee)* are connected by underwater passages harboring lake monsters. The lakes were formed by the collapse of underground cavities left after salt and gyp-sum deposits dissolved, opening holes that filled with water. The deepest plumbs out at 90 feet; however, the nearest thing to a lake monster is the puny cricket frog, a champion jumper but only 3 centimeters in length.

The Chihuahuan Desert harbors at least 100 species of birds, mammals, and reptiles, as well as a variety of drought-resistant plants. In Carlsbad, gardens at the **❼ Living Desert Zoological and Botanical State Park★** *(1504 Miehls Dr. 505-887-5516. Adm. fee)* represent animals and plants of various ecologies, including critters that normally venture out only after sunset, and a community of over 200 kinds of cactuses and succulents.

In Permian times (290 to 240 million years ago), much of what is now New Mexico lay beneath a tropical sea fringed with limestone reefs. Over 200 million years, the sea receded and the reefs were lifted, fractured, and buried under sediment. West of Whites City, water entering those fissures dissolved the limestone to create the famed labyrinth of **❽ Carlsbad Caverns National Park★★** *(Visitor Center 505-785-2232. Adm. fee).* One of the world's most extensive known cave systems, it is also among the most magnificent, with a myriad of formations along self-guided and ranger-led walking tours through well-lit but chilly (56°F) passageways and great rooms. Up top, a half-mile loop trail illustrates how different Chihuahuan Desert plants—the mescal heart of the agave in particular—fed, clothed, medicated, decorated, or otherwise served the Mescalero Apache. Near dusk from early May through October, thousands of Mexican free-tailed bats flutter from the cavern entrance to feed on flying insects.

The 50-mile-long Guadalupe range flanking US 62/180 to the west is part of the fossil reef giving rise to Carlsbad Caverns. Its southern wall juts into 86,416-acre **❾ Guadalupe Mountains National Park★** *(Visitor Center at Pine Springs 915-828-3251).* A 2.3-mile loop trail leads to Smith and Manzanita Springs and glades of fern, juniper, madrone, maple, and oak. The ruins of an 1858 stage-coach stop and an 1870s homestead are close by.

Southwest road maps abound with tiny symbols labeled "tanks," a term applied to places where rainwater collects naturally. (The Spanish called them *huecos,* or holes.) Ranging from cup-size depressions in rock to large ponds, they've been relied upon for water here for at least 10,000 years. Unexplained erosion processes created hundreds in **Hueco Tanks State Historical Park ★** *(915-857-1135. Adm. fee),* attracting farmers and nomadic hunters. They created thousands of pictographs, grouped in a dozen places along walking trails.

Highway US 62/180 becomes Montana Road as it enters **⑩ El Paso★** *(Visitor Center 915-534-0653. Mon.-Fri.)*, the largest city on the United States-Mexico border. Orient yourself with a panorama of El Paso, the Rio Grande, and neighboring Juárez, Mexico, from Arroyo Park on **Scenic Drive** and **Rim Road** *(Take Arizona Ave. NE from downtown to Alabama St., then turn left at Scenic Drive).*

The 12,000-year saga of local human history is the focus of the **Centennial Museum★** *(915-747-5565. Tues.-Sat.)* on the campus of the University of Texas at El Paso, west of town off Mesa Street. A NATIONAL GEOGRAPHIC article depicting lamaseries in Bhutan inspired the distinctive Himalayan style of the university's original buildings, erected in 1914.

Golden Spur Equestrian Drive Team, El Paso

The splendor of turn-of-the-century San Francisco provided the model for El Paso's grand **Paso del Norte Hotel** *(915-534-3000),* completed in 1912 at the downtown junction of El Paso, San Francisco, and Santa Fe Streets. The hotel's opulent marble Dome Bar gleams beneath a vaulted ceiling of beautiful Tiffany glass.

From the Civil War to the 1880s, Southwest settlers used adobe bricks, stone blocks, and large beams to build thick-walled haciendas with shaded porches. This combination of Spanish and European-American architecture has become known as Southwest territorial. There's a perfect example at the **Magoffin Homestead Historic Site★** *(1120 Magoffin Ave. Adm. fee).* The Magoffins moved their brood into the 19-room house here in 1875 (when it had only 7 rooms). Guided tours lead past the original family furnishings.

The **Concordia Cemetery★** on Yandell Drive (paralleling I-10 east of downtown) is El Paso's oldest. Headstones reflect an early ethnic diversity. Among those memorialized: gunfighter John Wesley Hardin (1853-1895), whose fast draw reputedly won 40 face-downs before a lawman shot first. Hardin's marker adjoins the west entrance to a walled section of Chinese graves.

● **570 miles** ● **3 to 4 days** ● **All year, but summer and fall are best.**

127

Unaware that Spain had claimed New Mexico for itself, Piro Indians welcomed Spanish settlers to their pueblo at what is now Soccoro. This central region, once scorched by volcanoes belching black lava, extended hospitality to early explorers who relied on its abundant game, seen in profusion at Bosque del Apache National Wildlife Refuge. Today, between the old cattle drive watering holes of Magdalena and Datil, radio astronomers at the Very Large Array Radio Telescope seek knowledge in radio noise from space. Tribal members at Zuni

Greater sandhill cranes, Bosque del Apache N.W.R.

Pueblo find wisdom in messages from spirits, while the centuries-old guest book that is Inscription Rock bears the mark of many who have made history in this region. Uranium brought prosperity to Grants, but little changes in the Sky City of Acoma, the last pueblo to surrender to Spanish rule. Prayers still echo in the pueblo mission surviving here, whereas only desert birds sing in the ruined naves of churches abandoned elsewhere.

Pictographs, Zuni Indian Reservation

In 1598 Don Juan de Oñate led a caravan of colonists from Mexico through the parched wilderness of sand and scrub on a 90-mile *jornada del muerto*—trail of the dead man—across a plain menaced by Apache raiders. Piro Indians welcomed the party to Pilabo Pueblo and gave them "much corn." Oñate established his colony nearby, naming the settlement ❶ **Soccoro** *(Chamber of Commerce, 103 Francisco de Avando. 505-835-0424)* in commemoration of the Piros' life-saving "succor."

The Chamber of Commerce publishes a walking tour guide to the **historic district** around Soccoro's downtown plaza, just west of California Street. The older neighborhoods here are a virtual encyclopedia of New Mexican architecture, from pueblo to territorial. Three blocks north of the plaza stands **San Miguel Mission** *(403 El Camino Real N.W. 505-835-1620),* where people have worshiped since 1821. The modest, twin-steepled adobe incorporates a wall from the original church, put up in 1628 but destroyed during the Pueblo Revolt of 1680.

Before heading west, take a side trip about 18 miles south where, come fall, more than 12,000 greater sandhill cranes descend upon the reedy wetlands of **Bosque del Apache National Wildlife Refuge** *(N. Mex. 1. 505-835-1828. Adm. fee).* They share the 57,000-acre refuge with an estimated 300 species of migratory and resident birds, including the rare whooping crane. A 15-mile-long loop road and four nature trails enter the peaceable kingdom.

Back in Soccoro, take US 60 west through **Magdalena,** a redbrick town that once made a good living as a mining, lumbering, and cattle-shipping hub. About 23 miles west, off N. Mex. 52, huge dish antennas at the **Very Large Array Radio Telescope★** *(505-835-7000)* observe radio noise emanating from deep space. Imaginative exhibits demonstrate the long reach of radio astronomy, explain its technology, and show images of galaxies, quasars, stars being born, and remnants of exploded stars.

Just west of the ranching town of Datil is the ❷ **Datil Well Campground** *(Off N. Mex. 60. 505-835-0412. Use fee),* a nice place to picnic. The old livestock watering hole has 22 campsites and free firewood. Sheep and cattle drives along the "hoof highway" from Springerville, Arizona, stopped here on their dusty shuffle to the Magdalena railhead.

From **Quemado,** another ranching hamlet on a lonely landscape of creaking windmills and far horizons, take N. Mex. 36 north into the **Zuni Indian Reservation.** To the west, N. Mex. 53 leads to ❸ **Zuni Pueblo** *(Tribal Headquarters, Main St. 505-782-4481),* one of the largest and most isolated of New Mexico's 19 pueblo communities. Visitors are welcome but must respect tribal rules of etiquette. (Read the information brochure!) Silversmiths and potters working here are among the most skilled in the entire Southwest.

The pueblo's church, **Nuestra Señora de Guadalupe de Zuni** (Our Lady of Guadalupe of Zuni), was dedicated in 1629, destroyed in the 1680 Pueblo Revolt, reopened in 1699, razed again in 1849, and reconstructed in 1968. Murals inside testify to the co-mingling of spiritual traditions: Zuni kachina dancers symbolizing the four seasons twirl and swoop across the plastered walls. The mission is usually locked, but a request at nearby St. Anthony's rectory *(505-782-4477)* may result in a private tour.

Backtrack on N. Mex. 53 and continue east to **El Morro National Monument★** *(505-783-4226. Adm. fee).* Since prehistoric times, travelers drinking from the freshwater pool here have left their mark in the soft red sandstone of the 200-foot-high bluff called **Inscription Rock.** Anasazi living in a pueblo atop the mesa chipped petroglyphs, but the first European to achieve immortality in writing here was the tireless Don Juan de Oñate. Newly

Coronado's Folly

Francisco Vásquez de Coronado was a young man on the rise when the viceroy of Mexico authorized him to search for Cibola, the fabled Seven Cities of Gold. Although the viceroy insisted that his purpose was "missionary," Coronado called it an "invasion of conquest." The contrast of intent is confirmed by the expedition's chronicler, who wrote that "such a noble body was never collected in the Indies," while a detractor described its professional soldiers as "vicious young men with nothing to do." They trekked from disappointment to disappointment on a 4,000-mile, two-year misadventure that reached Kansas. Coronado returned to Mexico City in the spring of 1542 in disgrace. He spent several years fighting charges of corruption and incompetence, and died in obscurity at the age of 44, 12 years after his return.

129

appointed as governor of Spain's New Mexico province, he signed his message *Pasó por aquí*—Passed by here, in 1605. Hundreds of others also passed by during the next 300 years, leaving graffiti in the styles of their day. A short, steep trail climbs to pueblo ruins capping the mesa.

Eastbound on N. Mex. 53 toward Grants, watch for signs to the **Ice Cave and Bandera Volcano** *(12000 Ice Caves Rd. 505-783-4303 or 888-ICE-CAVE. Adm. fee).* The 10,000-year-old volcanic lava tubes here contain perpetual ice formations (due to the 8,000-foot elevation and the insulating properties of solidified lava). Self-guiding trails explore the cave and 500-foot-high Bandera Volcano, a source of the region's lava beds.

Continue on N. Mex. 53, driving across volcanic landscapes to **El Malpais National Monument and National Conservation Area** *(505-783-4774).* The 376,000-acre preserve includes a 17-mile-long lava tube system, over 30 volcanoes, and New Mexico's largest freestanding natural arch. To reach the arch, drive south on N. Mex 117 (off I-40, past Grants), which skirts the jagged edge of the malpais, or badlands, lava flows.

Nobody paid attention to the little farming community of **Grants** *(Chamber of Commerce 505-287-4802 or 800-748-2142)* until 1950, when Navajo rancher Paddy Martinez found an odd yellow rock on nearby Haystack Mountain. The rock was uranium, from what turned out to be one of the world's richest lodes, touching off a 33-year boom that made life around here a lot easier.

Acoma potter at work

The story of America's Geiger counter giddiness is a nice counterpoint to 19th-century gold and silver rushes. (People behaved better this time around.) **The New Mexico Museum of Mining** *(100 Iron St. 505-287-4802 or 800-748-2142. Closed Sun. Oct.-April; adm. fee)* tells the story and gets to the heart of the matter—digging up the radioactive metal—in a mine display beneath the building. The uranium market lost its buzz in the 1980s, leaving half of America's reserves still in the ground here.

From Grants head east on I-40 to the exit for the ❹ **Pueblo of Acoma ★ ★** *(505-470-4966 or 800-747-0181. Closed for feast days in July and Oct., call ahead for info; adm. and photo fees).* Acoma have lived in the adobe Sky City since at least A.D. 1250—about 50 still do—and consider it the oldest continuously inhabited community in the

United States. Buses shuttle visitors up 367 feet to the mesa top, where guides lead tours among pueblo buildings positioned and terraced for maximum exposure to winter sunlight.

Acoma's twin-towered church, **San Esteban del Rey Mission★★,** is the largest of the early Southwestern missions. Completed in 1640 entirely from materials hauled

Pueblo of Acoma, inhabited for seven centuries

to the mesa top—roof beams were carried from Mount Taylor 20 miles north—the church has a nave nearly 50 feet high and walls 9 feet thick. Its fortresslike appearance, elegant simplicity, and lofty setting impart a striking dignity.

On the west side of Albuquerque, just north of I-40, five volcanic cinder cones rise above ➎ **Petroglyph National Monument ★★** *(4735 Unser Blvd. N.W. 505-839-4429. Adm. fee).* Stop and consider the more than 15,000 images chipped into West Mesa, a 17-mile-long volcanic escarpment of dark lava. The array spans about 3,000 years and include prehistoric, Spanish colonial, and territorial period images. Depictions include animals, birds, people, geometrics, and crosses.

Continue west on I-40 through Albuquerque (see Historical New Mexico drive, page 133), picking up N. Mex. 337 south at Tijeras. Drive though the pine and

131

juniper fringe of **Cibola National Forest** *(505-275-5207)* to where the route runs into N. Mex. 55. Take this south across the Estancia Valley to the ruins of **Quarai**★ *(505-847-2290),* the best preserved of the single Tiwa (Quarai) and two Tompiro (Abó and Gran Quivira) Indian farming villages comprising the **Salinas Pueblo Missions National Monument**★ *(Mountainair Visitor Center, US 60. 505-847-2585).* Remnants of low masonry walls reveal the

dimensions of the multistory, apartmentlike houses that once stood here. After about five years of construction ended in the 1630s, the red sandstone block walls of the pueblo's Franciscan church, **Nuestra Señora de la Purísima Concepción de Cuarac,** rose 40 feet on foundations 5 feet wide and 7 feet deep to become one of the most imposing missions in the Southwest. In 1677 drought, famine, and disease drove away

Ruins at Gran Quivira, Salinas Pueblo Missions National Monument

Spanish and Tiwa alike. The rustle of cottonwoods and the rubble of collapsed pueblos give the ruins a somber air of defeat and abandonment.

The ruins of **San Gregorio Mission** at nearby **Abó**★ *(US 60. 505-847-2400)* exhibit an unusual mix of medieval European church design and pueblo architecture. Construction of the reddish brown sandstone church took up the first half of the 17th century. The mission's rough walls rose 40 feet above the low adobes of the crowded farming village—a height intended to inspire awe.

The sprawling interlocking of foundations for residential rooms and ceremonial kivas at ➏ **Gran Quivira**★ *(N. Mex. 55 south of Mountainair. 505-847-2770)* distinguishes this prehistoric trade center. Perhaps as many as 3,000 people prospered here, in the largest of the Salinas pueblos, before they succumbed to thirst and disease in the 1670s. More ruins await excavation beneath dirt and cholla cactus, revealed by the waffle-iron pattern they impart to the desert. But the remains of two 17th-century Spanish churches, San Isidro and San Buenaventura, stand on the limestone hill in the company of juniper and pinyon at the edge of the south-trending desert.

● **480 miles** ● **4 to 5 days** ● **Drive to Chaco Canyon can be rough** ● **All year, but spring and fall are best.**

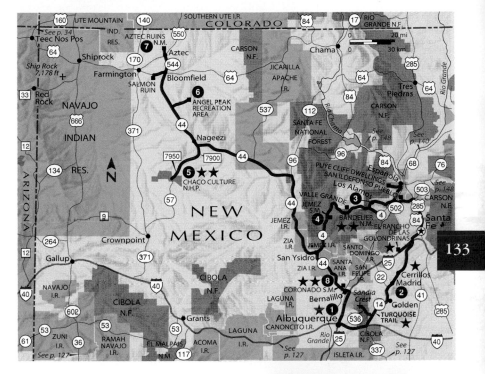

Under the watch of central New Mexico's Sandia Mountains, old Albuquerque preserves Spanish colonial architecture and culture, its superb museums and pueblo cultural center portraying the Southwest's European and Native American historical pageant. The world's longest single-span tramway crests Sandia Peak, overlooking the Turquoise Trail to Santa Fe, the last stop along the Camino Real from Mexico City. Settlers traded with the pueblos, and travelers still do, between visits to the ancient rock cities scattered across the region.

The modern sprawl of ❶ **Albuquerque ★** *(Visitors Bureau, 20 First Plaza S.W. 505-842-9918 or 800-284-2282)* surrounds an old town of unusual charm. In 1706 provincial governor Don Francisco Cuervo y Valdés settled some 12 to 20 families here, naming the villa after Mexico's viceroy, the duke of Alburquerque.

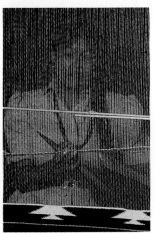

Navajo weaver, Old Town Albuquerque

New Mexico's third Spanish colony has lost an *r* but gained more than half a million people—a third of the state's population—making it the state's largest city.

The past is documented at the **Albuquerque Museum of Art and History**★ *(2000 Mountain Rd. N.W. 505-242-4600. Tues.-Sun.)*, one of North America's most extensive collections of Spanish colonial artifacts. Images in the photo archive portray local territorial-era life with the intimacy of a family album. The works of New Mexican artists are also exhibited, in the galleries and sculpture garden. The museum offers free guided walking tours of **Old Town Albuquerque.** This district of historic adobes, cafés, and shops in narrow streets, cobbled alleys, and tiny courtyards radiates from a tree-shaded central plaza dating from 1780. Native American artisans spread blankets along the plaza sidewalks to display silver-and-turquoise jewelry and other handicrafts. Wander on your own, or stop by the **Information Center** *(305 Romero St.)* for a map.

Annual International Balloon Fiesta, Albuquerque

134

Candles have flickered for nearly 300 years in **San Felipe de Neri Church**★ *(2005 N. Plaza N.W. 505-243-4628. Donations)*. High windows and 4-foot-thick walls provided physical as well as spiritual sanctuary during the city's rowdy youth. Nearby is the **Antonio Vigil House**★ *(413 Romero St.)*, a purebred Spanish colonial adobe. During the Civil War the elegant **Casa Armijo**★ *(San Felipe St.)* garrisoned Confederate troops, then Union soldiers.

A great stop for the whole family is the **New Mexico Museum of Natural History and Science**★ *(1801 Mountain Rd. N.W. 505-841-2800. Closed Mon. Jan. and Sept.; adm. fee)*. Electronic displays and multimedia exhibits—such as an "active" volcano spewing lava beneath a see-through floor—treat geology, paleontology, botany, and animal life with the high-tech showmanship of a theme park.

Southwest hikers keep a wary eye out for rattlesnakes,

which star at the **American International Rattlesnake
Museum** *(202 San Felipe N.W. 505-242-6569. Adm. fee)*, the
world's premier showcase for rattlers and things having to
do with the poisonous reptiles. Nearly two dozen slither
around in their re-created native habitats.

New Mexico has 19 pueblos, each of which possesses
a unique heritage manifested most visibly in art. To tell
their stories, the pueblos created the **Indian Pueblo
Cultural Center★** *(2401 12th St. N.W. 505-843-7270 or 800-
766-4405. Adm. fee)*, one of the Southwest's largest reposi-
tories of Native American arts and crafts. Each pueblo
maintains exhibits devoted to its own culture, enabling
visitors to see firsthand what distinguishes one tribe's art
from another's. Ceremonial dances are performed during
summer and on certain tribal holidays, and the center's
restaurant serves traditional cuisine.

Reminders of less-peaceful times are nearby. Ernie
Pyle's acclaimed combat reporting during World War II
won him a Pulitzer Prize and the home he built here in
1940 is now the **Ernie Pyle Branch Library** *(900 Girard
Blvd. S.E. 505-256-2065. Tues.-Sat.)*. The Cold War following
World War II is evoked at the **National Atomic Museum**
(Wyoming Blvd. and K St. 505-285-3243) on Kirtland Air
Force Base. Exhibits recount a half century of nuclear
research for war and peace.

You'd think it would be in Switzerland, but the world's
longest single-span tramway (a 2.7-mile arc of cable)
connects Albuquerque with 10,378-foot-high **Sandia
Peak,** east of town. You can
reach the summit by driving
the **Sandia Crest National
Scenic Byway** *(I-40 to N. Mex.
14 and 536)*, or by hiking the
8-mile La Luz trail up through
the Cibola National Forest. But
the **Sandia Peak Tramway** *(10
Tramway Loop N.E. 505-856-7325.
Fare)* takes only 15 silent
minutes to rise from desert to
alpine forest. The views along

Along the Turquoise Trail

the ride embrace a scenic 11,000 square miles.

Before I-25 linked Albuquerque and Santa Fe in a
no-frills way, everybody traveled between the two cities
on the scenic meander of N. Mex. 14 known as the

Inspired Amateurism

Credit the unusual charm
of the 17th-century New
Mexican churches to
inspired amateurism. So
far as is known, none of
the Franciscans who
oversaw their construction
were trained in architec-
ture. Using a few skilled
workers, the missionaries
instructed native laborers
based on memories of
churches in Mexico
and Spain. The result
had what a 17th-
century critic called "a certain barbaric splendor."

135

Turquoise Trail★. Many still prefer it for its string of old-time towns and their jewelry, gem, and handicraft shops. Photogenic **Golden,** which owes its name to an 1825 gold strike, has a lovely little adobe church. ❷ **Madrid** (pronounced MAD-drid), once a coal-mining town, has been revived by local artists, whose work is sold here. In the 1880s a mining boom kept pianos playing in the 21 saloons of drowsy **Cerrillos★,** which occasionally serves filmmakers as an Old West location.

In Spanish colonial days the lonely trail between Mexico City and Santa Fe—El Camino Real, the Royal Road—was the only link between colonial settlements. Oxcart caravans made the 1,600-mile journey in three months, squeaking along on wooden axles greased with animal fat. Their last stop before Santa Fe was the village of **El Rancho de las Golondrinas★** (334 Los Pinos Rd. 505-471-2261. June-Sept. or by appt.; adm. fee), where travelers could stretch, wash up, enjoy a cooked meal, and sleep on leather cots. The village preserves the hacienda, general store, and blacksmith shop, along with other old-time workplaces. Volunteer docents in period clothing work as Spanish-Mexican colonists did in the 17th and 18th centuries.

Pumpkin harvest, El Rancho de las Golondrinas

San Ildefonso Pueblo (Visitor Center, N. Mex. 502. 505-455-3549. Photo. & sketching fees), northwest of Santa Fe (see Santa Fe Loop drive, page 140), is renowned for its pottery. And probably no individual Pueblo artist is found in more Southwest museums than Maria Martinez, who in the 1920s revived San Ildefonso's unique style of black-on-black pottery. Shops sell the work of artists continuing the Martinez tradition, as well as other distinctive styles.

Eleven miles north, on the Santa Clara Indian Reservation, the mile-long **Puye Cliff Dwellings and Communal**

Traditional Native American foods, San Ildefonso Pueblo

House Ruins *(505-753-7326. Adm. fee)* once rose three stories high inside cliff-wall caves. An estimated 740 rooms sheltered members of an ancestral Puebloan farming village between A.D. 1100 and the late 1500s.

Like this ancient tribe, who hid their villages from enemies, the U.S. government in 1943 kept secret the establishment of nearby ❸ **Los Alamos** *(505-662-8105 or 800-444-0707)*. The mesa-top community of scientists and engineers, initially dedicated to the development of the atomic bomb, still devotes most of its annual billion-dollar-plus budget to issues of national security. Today the staff of the Los Alamos National Laboratory—a 2,224-building complex spread over 43 square miles—focuses on stockpile stewardship, ensuring the safety and reliability of those weapons remaining in the national arsenal. For a taste of what else they're up to, visit the lab's popular **Bradbury Science Museum**★★ *(15th St. and Central Ave. 505-667-4444)*. Over 40 interactive displays recount the Manhattan Project which produced the world's first A-bombs, and provide an overview of research into such things as solar, geothermal, and nuclear energy.

137

During World War II the log-built dining hall and dormitory of the Los Alamos Ranch School for Boys was filled with scientists; today the **Fuller Lodge Art Center and Gallery** *(2132 Central Ave. 505-662-9331. Closed Sun. Nov.-March)* uses it to show the work of area artists. Regional Native American artifacts and a photographic and artifact record of wartime life here are permanently displayed in the adjacent **Los Alamos County Historical Museum** *(1921 Juniper St. 505-662-4493)*. Among the outdoor exhibits stand a 13th-century Tewa ruin and a reassembled homesteader's cabin.

People known as Anasazi left hundreds of ancestral

Bandelier National Monument

Pueblo sites dating up to the mid-1500s on the mesa tops and eroded volcanic rock canyons of **Bandelier National Monument★★** *(505-672-3861. Adm. fee).* The almost roadless, 50-square-mile park is a natural, geological, and archaeological wonderland, with 70 miles of trails through a series of sheer-walled canyons, some as deep as 600 feet. Trails begin from the Visitor Center, located along tree-shaded Frijoles Creek near Tyuonyi, a two-story pueblo built seven centuries ago. A major fire in the spring of 1996 temporarily closed the backcountry and will continue to affect the wilderness for years to come.

138

Pueblo Bonito ruins, Chaco Culture National Historical Park

N. Mex. 4 winds west along a scenic loop that inclines through Santa Fe National Forest to **Valle Grande,** a verdant mountain bowl that is part of a volcanic caldera 12 miles in diameter. From the air it looks like a circular depression.

By 1630 the San José de los Jemez mission church and monastery in ❹ **Jemez State Monument** *(505-829-3530. Adm. fee)* was withering from lack of converts. The ruined sandstone church stands on a pueblo site called Guisewa, at least three centuries older. Archaeologists still have much to do here, but some of what they've already found is displayed in a small museum.

South from N. Mex. 44, the veil draping the Anasazi world is lifting, thanks in good part to recent research in and around ❺ **Chaco Culture National Historical Park★★** *(505-786-7014. Adm. fee).* The 17-mile-long, mile-wide canyon contains 17 major pueblos and over 400 smaller dwellings dating from A.D. 900, including one of the largest excavated prehistoric ruins in North America. The sight of **Pueblo Bonito★★**, a D-shaped structure of

800 rooms covering 3 acres of Chaco Canyon, quickens the heart. Trail maps, available at the Visitor Center, guide you through the ruins, where mysteries still abound. One puzzle: roads constructed with precision, sometimes 30 feet wide, from here to Utah and Colorado. Their purpose is unknown. When accessing the park, keep in mind that the road from near Nageezi (County Road 7900) is mainly dirt, rough in all weather, and impassable when wet—so use caution.

Ship Rock, Navajo reservation

Northbound again on N. Mex. 44, you'll near the turn-off to the **6** **Angel Peak Recreation Area** *(505-599-8900)*, a lofty region of unusual sandstone formations, multi-colored canyons, and eroded landforms at the base of 6,991-foot-high Angel Peak.

To the northwest, George Salmon and subsequent owners kept treasure hunters from looting the county-owned **Salmon Ruin,** 2 miles west of Bloomfield. The 2-acre site preserves a two-story, 450-foot-long, C-shaped masonry complex and more than a *million* artifacts recovered from the late 11th-century Chaco settlement. Many are on display at the adjoining **San Juan County Museum Association, Research Center, and Library at Salmon Ruin** *(6131 US 64. 505-632-2013. Adm. fee).*

Pioneers who knew more about sod busting than history misnamed the 500-room rock-and-timber Anasazi pueblo at **7** **Aztec Ruins National Monument** *(505-334-6174. Adm. fee).* Its massively buttressed, 12th-century underground ceremonial room, the Great Kiva, was reconstructed by archaeologists in the 1930s, enabling visitors to enter a ritual space seldom seen by non-Indians. The Pueblo farmers spent about 200 years here before leaving the site in 1300. Some of what they left behind is displayed in the Visitor Center museum.

Backtrack along N. Mex. 44 to San Ysidro and continue south to where Coronado (see sidebar page 129) led his weary caballeros in the fall of 1540, on his quest for the seven golden cities of Cibola. He is believed to have spent two winters encamped in the Kuaua Pueblo at **8** **Coronado State Monument**★★ *(425 Coronado Rd. off N. Mex. 44. 505-867-5351. Adm. fee).* An interpretive trail winds through the ruin to a restored kiva with re-created wall murals depicting rain dances, hunting, and fertility rituals. The original murals, as rare as they are fragile, are preserved in the gallery.

Ship Rock

Is there any wonder that towering Ship Rock is sacred to the Navajo? Tribal myth and lore swirl around the jagged, 1,500-foot-high pinnacle, whose Navajo name is *tse bit'a'i,* the rock with wings. The eroded core of a volcano pierced the earth's crust 30 million years ago and stands today at over 7,000 feet. The slanted escarpment racing away from the spire was formed when solidifying magma pushed up through a mammoth fissure and hardened. Reservation Route 33 to Red Rock skirts the landmark, but Tribal Council permission *(505-368-1081 or 368-1085)* is required to approach it. Climbing is never allowed.

139

● **460 miles** ● **4 to 5 days** ● **All year, though spring and fall are best** ● **"Monsoons" in July and August can bring brief showers daily** ● **Good roads throughout, but winter snows can close mountain passes.**

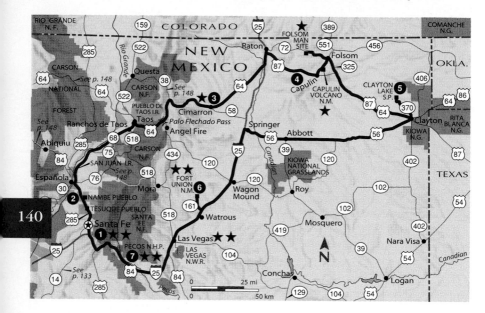

140

Santa Fe is America's second oldest city and the chief guardian of New Mexico's cherished multicultural heritage. Nearby, Tesuque and Nambe Pueblos keep a foot firmly planted in prehistory; Cimarron and Raton can look back no further than Wild West days. Stone spearpoints found near Folsom proved hunters roamed this region 10,000 years ago. Fort Union protected Santa Fe Trail travelers until the railroads replaced covered wagons and turned watering holes into prosperous cities like Las Vegas, still decorated by its 19th-century Victorian buildings. Seasonal changes bring migratory birds back to area marshlands, but nothing will return life to the ruins of Pecos, perhaps the greatest Southwest pueblo community ever, a casualty of Spanish colonial zeal.

In 1610 provincial governor Don Pedro de Peralta established his new capital at 7,000 feet in the foothills of the Sangre de Cristo Mountains, making ❶ **Santa Fe ★ ★** *(Visitor Center 505-984-6760 or 800-777-2489),* the oldest seat of government in the United States. Peralta's adobe headquarters in the **Palace of the Governors ★** *(505-827-6483.*

Tues.-Sun.; adm. fee) forms the northern perimeter of Santa Fe's historical **Plaza**★ and has been in public service longer than any building in America.

Santa Fe's first and finest pueblo revival building is the nearby **Museum of Fine Arts**★★ *(107 W. Palace Ave. 505-827-4468. Tues.-Sun.; adm. fee. Note: Many Santa Fe museums are affiliated, offering four-day entrance passes to all)*, setting the standard for the style since 1917. The regional art exhibited here includes many works by Georgia O'Keeffe and stars from the Santa Fe and Taos art colonies. Portions of its huge photography collection are also on display.

According to legend, prayer brought about the completion of the French Romanesque **Loretto Chapel**★ *(211 Old Santa Fe Trail. 505-984-7971. Adm. fee)*, just south of the Plaza. Its French architect modeled the church after Paris's Sainte Chapelle, and French and Italian stonemasons began work in 1873. But the designer died without completing stairs to the choir loft, leaving Loretto's Catholic sisters to beseech God. In 1877 an aged, bearded carpenter arrived on a donkey and built the Miraculous Staircase, which spirals upward without a center pole. He then disappeared without requesting payment.

141

Santa Fe, below the Sangre de Cristo Mountains

Nearby **St. Francis Cathedral** *(231 Cathedral Pl. 505-982-5619)*, a French Romanesque edifice begun in 1869, reflects the taste of French-born archbishop Jean-Baptiste Lamy, who energized New Mexican Catholicism from Santa Fe by riding from church to church. He's buried beneath the altar, watched over by perhaps the oldest representation of the Madonna in North America, and enjoying a secular immortality as the model for Willa Cather's novel *Death Comes for the Archbishop.*

Statue in front of State Capitol Building

A walk to **Santuario Nuestra Señora de Guadalupe**★★ *(100 Guadalupe St. 505-988-2027. May-Oct. Mon.-Sat., Nov.-April Mon.-Fri.),* three blocks southwest of the Plaza, takes you through the shops and restaurants of the **Guadalupe Historic District**★. The California mission-style church, built between 1776 and 1796, has survived revolution, fire, and atrocious remodeling (at one point into a New England-style schoolhouse). The museum exhibits 17th-century paintings and a photographic church history.

Follow the Santa Fe River east to the **State Capitol Building** *(Old Santa Fe Trail and Paseo de Peralta. 505-986-4589. Mem. Day–Labor Day Mon.-Sat., Labor Day–Mem. Day Mon.-Fri.).* Its circular design was inspired by the Pueblo people's Zia sun symbol (also on the state flag), representing the four compass points, the seasons, and four stages of life.

Just down the street stands the **San Miguel Mission**★★ *(401 Old Santa Fe Trail. 505-983-3974).* The little church was Santa Fe's first, and a circa 1628 document accusing New Mexico's governor of "impious conduct during the Mass" establishes it as North America's oldest church structure. Wooden rafters (called vigas), as thick as telephone poles, support its high ceilings. One of the oldest neighborhoods in the United States is just around the corner, the **Barrio d'Analco,** where houses date from the early 1600s.

Santa Fe is one of the most active art markets in the country. Much of that business takes place on **Canyon Road** *(E off Paseo de Peralta).* The old Indian trail looks down-at-the-heel in places, but many of the city's leading galleries, restaurants, and craft shops line the narrow pavement.

At the top of Canyon Road is **Cristo Rey Church**★★ *(1120 Canyon Rd. 505-983-8528),* a perfect expression of pueblo revival architecture and the largest adobe building in the United States. Don't be disappointed that it dates only from 1940, for no Southwest church was built with more loving attention to traditional details. Parishioners made the 150,000 bricks of mud and straw used in its construction.

The sanctuary features an ornate, 18th-century carved stone altar screen, orphaned when a Spanish Colonial-era military chapel on the Plaza was razed. It weighs 250 tons.

To visit three of Santa Fe's most interesting museums, take the Old Santa Fe Trail about 2 miles south from the Plaza, following museum signs to Camino Lejo. Fortunately for the rest of us, Florence Dibell Bartlett collected folk art—costumes, pottery, metalwork, carvings—whatever people around the world made from whimsy, wood, and everything else. She donated a museum and her 4,500-piece collection to New Mexico, founding the **Museum of International Folk Art**★★ *(706 Camino Lejo. 505-827-6350. Tues.-Sun.; adm. fee)* in 1953. In 1978 a kindred soul bequeathed 106,000 items, confirming the museum's status as the world's premier showcase of things made by hand to amuse, instruct, and simply decorate. You'll never forget this place.

The adjoining **Wheelwright Museum of the American Indian**★★ *(704 Camino Lejo. 505-982-4636. Donations)* mimics the circular shape of a Navajo hogan. Exhibits run the gamut of art types to present the highest levels of creative achievement in Native American communities. The museum store re-creates the look of an old-time Southwest trading post.

Contemporary artistic trends among New Mexico's Pueblo, Navajo, and Apache

Indian tradespeople, Palace of the Governors, Santa Fe Plaza

people regularly refresh exhibits at the **Museum of Indian Arts and Culture**★ *(710 Camino Lejo. 505-827-6344. Tues.-Sun.; adm. fee)*. Artists demonstrate their craft and discuss the traditions represented in their work.

Northbound on US 84/285 from Santa Fe, you'll soon see the eroded sandstone formations marking **Tesuque**

New Mexico 21, near Cimarron

Pueblo *(505-983-2667)*, where Tewa-speaking people have lived since A.D. 1200. The village played a leading role in the 1680 Pueblo Revolt and is still strongly attached to its aboriginal heritage. People travel from afar to nearby ❷ **Nambe Pueblo** *(N. Mex. 4. 505-455-2036)* for the silver jewelry and pottery sold here, along with Nambe's trademark cooking pots of sparkling mica-rich clay. About two dozen of the pueblo's pre-20th-century adobes survive.

Drive to Taos (see Taos Drive, page 148), then turn east on US 64. This road climbs through **Carson National Forest** *(505-758-6390)* to 9,101-foot Palo Flechado Pass, dropping into the grassland basin of **Moreno Valley** near the ski resort town of **Angel Fire** *(Chamber of Commerce 505-377-6661 or 800-446-8117)*.

America's first monument to those who served in Vietnam rises on a knoll just north of the junction of US 64 and N. Mex. 434. The small chapel of the **DAV Vietnam Veterans National Memorial** ★ *(505-377-6900. May-Sept. Tues.-Sun., Oct.-April Wed.-Sun.)*, dedicated in 1971, was built by a local family mourning the loss of a soldier son.

Wheel ruts score the terrain where the **Santa Fe Trail** passes west of ❸ **Cimarron** ★ *(Chamber of Commerce 505-376-2417)*. From the late 1860s to about 1880, the town had quite a reputation for gunplay—more than two dozen murders took place at the **St. James Hotel** *(505-376-2664)*, opened in 1880 and refurbished to its original style (but keeping the bullet holes in the dining room ceiling).

Colfax County history is the focus of the **Old Aztec Mill Museum** *(595-376-2913. May Sat.-Sun., June-Aug. Fri.-Wed.; adm. fee)*, a four-story brick pile put up in 1864 by land tycoon Lucien Maxwell, who founded Cimarron in 1848 as the base of his 1.7-million-acre empire. The gristmill is full of old clothing, photographs, Native American artifacts, antique furniture, and historical curios.

Maxwell's domain reached to **Raton** *(Chamber of Commerce 505-445-3689)*, a pleasant town built by coal mining, railroading, and ranching. Exhibits at the **Raton Museum** *(216 S. First St. 505-445-8979. Wed.-Sat.)* concentrate on those enterprises. The city has about 70 vintage buildings and publishes a walking tour guide to the **Raton Historical District,** centering around First and Second Streets.

The mesas around ❹ **Capulin** are capped with lava from eruptions ending about 62,000 years ago. The thousand-foot cinder cone of **Capulin Volcano National Monument★** *(505-278-2201. Adm. fee)* is one of the country's most symmetrical. The 2-mile drive to the rim brings you to 8,120 feet and views embracing five states. Those faint lines to the southeast are old wagon tracks, from a supply route to Fort Union.

Continue north on N. Mex. 325 to **Folsom,** then take N. Mex. 72 west to the **Folsom Man Site★.** Here in 1926 excavation began on a site where ranch foreman George McJunkin found chipped stone points among bones newly exposed by erosion in Dead Horse Gulch. Archaeologists identified them as extinct bison skeletons and recovered 19 projectile points that established a human presence in North America going back at least 9,500 years. (Conventional wisdom then said 4,000 years.) A small museum exhibits replicas of Folsom points and tools.

Clayton *(Chamber of Commerce 505-374-9253)* was established in the mid-1880s as a cattle-shipping point and is still at it, earning extra money by extracting carbon dioxide from nearby Bravo Dome, said to be the world's largest reserve. Check out the dining room and bar of the **Eklund Hotel** *(15 Main St. 505-374-2551)*, built in 1892 and little changed. Clayton's weekly cattle auction is interesting to watch as buyers from five states bid for the beef.

Christmas Welcome

A Christmas holiday ritual unique to the Southwest is the placement of *luminarias,* or paper lanterns—candles anchored in sand-filled brown paper sacks—along the streets, sidewalks, walls, and rooflines of adobe houses. Known as *farolitos,* "little lanterns," they are set out to welcome Santo Niño, the Christ child. Medieval Spanish tradition called for welcoming fires to burn throughout the holidays, but in the colonial Southwest the scarcity of wood made that impossible. The opening of the Santa Fe Trail and the introduction of long-burning candles and paper sacks from the East led to the creation of the farolito, thousands of which set the Southwest aglow every December.

145

Dinosaurs once roamed 12 miles northwest of town (via N. Mex. 370), leaving their fearsome footprints at what is now ❺ **Clayton Lake State Park** *(505-374-8808. Adm. fee).* There are so many, in fact, it looks as if they danced a fandango. Follow signs along a half-mile trail to the 100-million-year-old tracks, discovered in the early 1980s.

Before hooking west, drive a few miles east of Clayton on US 64 to the **Kiowa National Grasslands** *(505-374-9652).* The West was once thickly tufted with tall native bunchgrass, now nearly erased by farming and the dust storms of the 1930s. Preserves like this resemble primordial North American prairies. There aren't any signs; just look for greenish clumps on the landscape.

Begun in 1879, the imposing Second Empire county courthouse in **Springer** *(Chamber of Commerce 505-483-2998)* houses the **Santa Fe Trail Museum** *(6th St. and Maxwell Ave. Mem. Day–Labor Day; adm. fee),* which focuses on everyday 19th-century pioneer life, poignantly evoked by ordinary things like clothes, cooking utensils, and furniture.

In territorial days, meat brokering was a lucrative trade, and the area's most sought-after account was the Army's garrison at ❻ **Fort Union National Monument**★★ *(N. Mex. 161 off I-25. 505-425-8025. Adm. fee).* Established in 1851 to protect the Santa Fe Trail from Indian attack, the forlorn expanse of freestanding chimneys, stone foundations, and crumbled adobe ruins was at one time the biggest military base in the Southwest. Exhibits in the territorial-style Visitor Center include historical maps and interesting military and trail memorabilia.

The Atchison, Topeka & Santa Fe Railroad's arrival in 1879 transformed the water hole at **Las Vegas**★★ *(Chamber of Commerce 505-425-8631 or 800-832-5947)* into New Mexico's primary shipping terminus and largest city. In the early 1900s the AT&SF constructed shorter routes across the state, diverting traffic from Las Vegas, which went bust. Poverty made urban renewal impossible, resulting in *five* historic districts with over 900 buildings listed on the National Register of Historic Places. There are so many styles of architecture here—adobe, Victorian, and territorial—that you really should spend an hour cruising the neighborhoods. The **Downtown Plaza District**★★ has

Christo Rey Church, northwest of Las Vegas

adobes from prerailroad days. Use the city's free guide to buildings here and along Bridge Street, a block east.

Why is the **Rough Riders Memorial** *(725 N. Grand Ave. 505-425-8726. Mon.-Fri.)* in Las Vegas? Because in 1899 Teddy Roosevelt attended a reunion of his Spanish-American War buddies at the Castaneda Hotel here. The memorial has souvenirs from T.R.'s Cuban adventure, which made him a national hero.

Though an avid hunter, Teddy championed federal protection for prairie wet-lands like those in the 8,700-acre **Las Vegas National Wildlife Refuge** *(505-425-3581).* Its proximity to the Continental Divide attracts

Pueblo ruins, Pecos National Historic Park

thousands of migratory birds from both the western and eastern United States—at least 244 species, including Canada geese, sandhill cranes, and bald eagles—which use the reedy haven as a rest stop. A 7-mile scenic drive probes the watery wilderness. The mile-long nature trail affords a close encounter with birds and beasts (such as coyote), but requires a permit from the refuge office.

Coronado's log described the "nearly 500 warriors" of the fortresslike pueblo at ❼ **Pecos National Historical Park**★★ *(Off I-25. 505-757-6414. Adm. fee)* as "feared throughout the land." Called Cicuye by the Spanish, the red stone community peaked in the mid-15th century as the Southwest's preeminent pueblo trading center, where Rio Grande Valley pueblos bartered with nomadic hunters from the Great Plains. About 2,000 people occupied an apartment-like complex of some 1,000 rooms reaching five stories. Disease and hostile tribes reduced its population to 17 in 1838, when the survivors emigrated to join the Jemez Pueblo. Stop by the Visitor Center first; the interpretive information and short film will make your stroll through the pueblo and mission ruins much more meaningful.

147

● 320 miles ● 3 to 4 days ● All year, but spring wildflowers and autumn color add special pleasure to those seasons ● Good roads throughout ● Winter snow, icy pavement, and fog can make the High Road to Taos treacherous. N. Mex. 38 between Eagle Nest and Questa may be closed in winter.

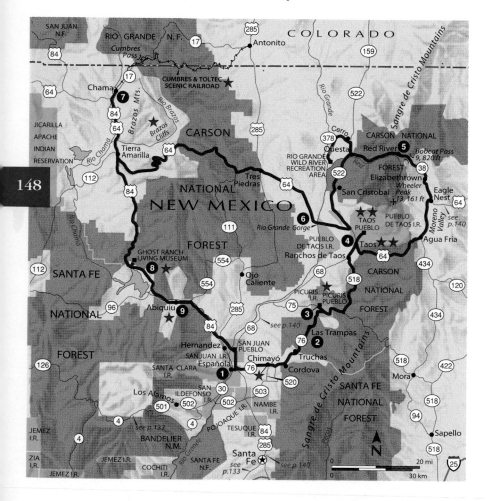

Time moves slowly in northern New Mexico's Hispanic highlands, where past and present overlap in rural villages like Chimayó, Cordova, Truchas, and Las Trampas. The Taos art colony approaches its centennial with fanfare, while Taos Pueblo, perhaps a thousand years old, no longer counts the years. The Sangre de Cristo Mountains and the Moreno Valley draw hunters, fishermen, and winter sports

enthusiasts. Red River stages Old West pageants, and a
coal-fired train from Chama travels tracks of the past. Not
yet a border, the Rio Grande cuts a deep gorge through
sagebrush desert, while the braided Rio Chama waters the
red rock country that inspired painter Georgia O'Keeffe.

❶ **Española** *(Chamber of Commerce 505-753-2831)* takes
its name from San Gabriel de los Españoles, which was
founded in 1598 as New Mexico's first capital. It soon lost
the honor to nearby Santa Fe, but retains its strong Native

Ranchos de Taos Church of San Francisco de Asís, near Taos

American and Hispanic roots. Española's folk art fleet of
low-slung, ornately customized cars makes it the self-
proclaimed Low Rider Capital of the World.

From Española, N. Mex. 76 joins the
scenic High Road to Taos. The route winds
through eroded high desert and cottonwood
valleys to **Chimayó★,** whose Hispanic
weaving families specialize in vividly
colored clothing and blankets. Each year,
thousands of believers flock to **El Santuario
de Chimayó★** *(505-351-4889)*, the Lourdes
of the Southwest, seeking cures from hand-
fuls of sacred earth scooped from within the
church. Sit in a rear pew to admire the interior, a masterpiece of Spanish colonial religious decoration.

Taos gallery owner with pine needle basket

The bishop authorizing the people of ❷ **Las Trampas**
to build **San José de Gracia★** exhorted them to strive for
"seemliness and cleanliness." In 1760 they completed a
twin-towered church whose facade is among the most

Storefronts in Red River

150

dignified of any in New Mexico. With about 350 residents today, ❸ **Picuris Pueblo**★ *(505-587-2519. Tour and photography fees)* is among the smallest of New Mexico's 19 Pueblo communities, yet one of its most hospitable. Turn left onto N. Mex. 75 and follow the signs. The pueblo's restaurant serves tribal fare, and the free museum is a place to admire prehistoric artifacts and buy contemporary versions. The humble **San Lorenzo Church,** the fifth on this site, is a copy of the original, which was burned during the Pueblo's 1680 uprising against Spanish rule.

Many first-time visitors to the **Taos Plateau** are confused by the fact that three communities here share the name Taos: the 1,000-year-old Pueblo de Taos; Spanish colonial Taos, christened Don Fernando de Taos in 1710; and Ranchos de Taos, a Taos Pueblo farming annex established prior to the arrival of European settlers.

Approaching from the south, N. Mex. 68 and 518 merge in Ranchos de Taos and pass the **Church of San Francisco de Asís**★★ *(505-758-2754. Adm. fee).* Painters Georgia O'Keeffe and John Marin and photographers Ansel Adams and Paul Strand, captivated by the massive buttresses and walls at the rear of the sanctuary, have helped make this one of the most recognized images of the Southwest. Before you enter the circa 1815 church, visit the parish hall to watch a video about its history.

Still south of the town of Taos, turn onto Ranchitos Road and follow signs to the best preserved, late northern New Mexico colonial-era house in the Southwest: **La Hacienda de Don Antonio Severina Martinez**★★ *(505-758-1000. Adm. fee).* The 21-room adobe, filled with period furnishings, looks as it did upon completion in the early 1800s. Thick windowless walls protected the Martinez clan from marauding Apache, Navajo, and Ute resisting the influx of Spanish-Mexican settlers. A sheltered life in the sun was made possible by the hacienda's two courtyards.

The best way to explore ❹ **Taos**★★ *(Visitor Center 505-758-3837 or 800-732-TAOS)* is on foot, starting with the

Taos's Old Glory

It is customary to lower the American flag at sunset. In Taos, however, Old Glory flies above the plaza day and night. During the Civil War, Southern sympathizers living in the village repeatedly took down the Stars and Stripes. Union loyalists, including Kit Carson, cut and trimmed the tallest tree they could find, nailed the flag to it, put it up on the square, and posted two riflemen to keep it there. The incident inspired Congress to forever grant Taos the unusual privilege of flying the national banner around the clock, in recognition of its patriotism.

Taos Plaza. The handsome stucco rectangle embraces galleries, bookstores, and shops selling all kinds of unusual and handmade crafts.

It would be hard to find an adobe dwelling more appealing than the **Blumenschein Home**★★ *(222 Ledoux St. 505-758-0505. Adm. fee),* two blocks southwest of the plaza. Taos Society of Artists co-founder Ernest Blumenschein and his artist wife bought it in 1919, made additions, and filled it with handmade Taos and European furniture. It's a shrine to Blumenschein creativity (even their daughter wielded a brush), with more art per square foot than most galleries. Burt Harwood, another early patron of the Taos art circle, lived with his wife in a handsome house that's now the **Harwood Foundation Library and Museum**★★ *(238 Ledoux St. 505-758-9826. Mon.-Sat.; adm. fee).* Paintings here illustrate the styles of art associated with Taos. Look for a gorgeous collection of wooden saints, or santos, made by early Spanish carvers.

Follow Kit Carson Road (US 64) east from the plaza to the 12-room **Kit Carson Home and Museum**★ *(505-758-4741. Adm. fee).* Christopher Carson—mountain man, trapper, Army scout, Union colonel during the Civil War, steely enforcer in the gathering of Navajo into camps—was 33 when he married 14-year-old Josefa Jaramillo, the daughter of a wealthy Taos family. Carson gave her the house as a wedding present. It's full of mountain-manly

151

Rio Grande National Wild and Scenic River

Ghost Ranch high country

gear, historical documents, artifacts, and antiques. Kit and Josefa are buried in nearby **Kit Carson Park** *(505-758-4160),* a 20-acre wooded expanse of green just north off Paseo del Pueblo Norte.

Up the street is one of Taos's most interesting homes, created by a Russian émigré artist, Nicolai Fechin. He embellished the antique adobe with Russian-style woodwork, preserved today by the **Fechin Institute ★★** *(227 Paseo del Pueblo Norte. 505-758-1710. Mem. Day–Oct. Tues.-Sun.; adm. fee).* Exhibits recall the painter's innovative spirit as a mentor and teacher. A few blocks away stands another preserved residence, now the **Governor Bent Museum** *(117A Bent St. 505-758-2376. Adm. fee).* The rough-hewn adobe is where, in 1847, territorial governor Charles Bent was killed by a mob protesting New Mexico's annexation by the United States. The stolid building is a somber repository of artifacts going back to prehistoric Indian times.

Taos Pueblo ★★ *(505-758-9593. Adm. fee, plus fees for photography, sketching, and filming)* is five minutes north of town and a thousand years removed. Park on the broad plaza between two sprawling, multistory adobe buildings (North House and South House), built between A.D. 1000 and 1450. Signs invite you into craft and curio shops and bakeries selling bread baked in small earthen outdoor ovens. About 2,000 tribal members live outside the pueblo on reservation land, while the 200 or so who live here forsake electricity and running water. Inside the pueblo's **Church of San Gerónimo ★**, a painting of the Virgin Mary surrounded by a halo of golden corncobs

illustrates the community's spiritual duality. The chapel was built about 1850 to replace an earlier church destroyed during the Mexican-American War.

Standard Oil heiress Millicent Rogers came to New Mexico in 1947, fell in love with everything about it, and began to collect the best examples of Native American and Hispanic art she could find. Her collection, perhaps the finest in the world, is housed 4 miles north of Taos in the adobe-style **Millicent Rogers Museum** ★★ *(N. Mex. 522 off US 64. 505-758-2462. Closed Mon. Nov.-April; adm. fee).* For a scenic circular drive, take US 64 east from Taos through Carson National Forest to the **Moreno Valley** (see page 144). New Mexico's highest peak, 13,161-foot **Mount Wheeler,** looms darkly to the west.

Sandstone walls rising west of the highway, just north of Eagle Nest, are remnants of the Mutz Hotel in long-dead **Elizabethtown,** which sprang up in 1868 following a gold strike along Willow Creek. A dirt road from the highway passes by small ranches to reach the ruin, which is photogenic but without interpretive information.

You can coast most of the way down from 9,820-foot **Bobcat Pass,** the spine of the Sangre de Cristo Mountains, to ❺ **Red River** *(Chamber of Commerce 505-754-2366 or 800-348-6444).* This old mining outpost has become a mountain-country recreation spot and living history Old West town. There are streamside campgrounds west of town in the **Red River Canyon,** where you can picnic to the rush of water amid the rustle of quaking aspen.

N. Mex. 38 west through the Sangre de Cristos to Questa crosses broad grasslands and forests. If you follow the Red River to its meeting with the Rio Grande, you'll find yourself in a narrow gorge looking up 650 feet at a strip of sky in the heart of the **Rio Grande Wild River Recreation Area** *(Visitor Center 505-758-8851).* For an impressive view into the chasm, take N. Mex. 522 north from Questa 3 miles, turn left at signs pointing west to the village of **Cerro,** and continue 3 more miles, taking the road's right fork to mesa-like **La Junta Point.** There are

---

Ghost Ranch

Heading south on US 84, you'll pass through the eroded red rock landscapes that captivated artist Georgia O'Keeffe in 1934 on her first visit to **Ghost Ranch** *(505-685-4333).* Nearby canyons were reputedly haunted by howling witches, but when O'Keeffe saw the old Spanish homestead, she heard the siren call of her own destiny as a painter. She bought a cottage here in 1940 and took emotional ownership of everything else. Of a distant butte she said, "It belongs to me. God told me if I painted it enough, I could have it." Nothing material remains of O'Keeffe. Ghost Ranch is now a United Presbyterian Church adult study and conference center, 21,000 acres of desert solitude open to all, with lodging, seminars, and field study programs. The **Ruth Hall Museum of Anthropology** *(Closed Mon.)* is a re-creation of a Spanish ranch house with interpretive exhibits of Indian pottery and other crafts. The adjoining **Florence Hawley Museum of Paleontology** *(Closed Mon.)* contains dinosaur and fossil finds.

campsites, picnic tables, and a nature trail on the canyon rim among sagebrush and centuries-old pinyon trees. Five trails—short but steep—descend to the river, where pines grow. The 0.8-mile Big Arsenic Springs Trail leads to petroglyphs chipped into boulders.

Take N. Mex. 522 south past San Cristobal and head west on US 64. What first looks like a bluff on the desert ahead is the west wall of the **6** **Rio Grande Gorge.** Parking areas on both sides of the span across the chasm afford good, dizzying, views down to the fast-flowing river.

The highway between **Tres Piedras** and **Tierra Amarilla** is one of New Mexico's most scenic, threading the **Brazos Mountains,** where grassland basins and forests of evergreen and aspen at 10,000 feet are so cleanly delineated they look like landscaping. The **Brazos Cliffs** ★, composed of 1.7- to 1.8-billion-year-old Precambrian quartzite (the cliffs contain the oldest known rock in New Mexico), plunge 2,000 feet to the Rio Chama Valley.

In 1880 the Denver & Rio Grande Railroad laid a spur line southwest to link the San Juan mining region with Denver, Colorado, and eastern markets. New Mexico and Colorado now own the refurbished 64-mile route

Taos Pueblo, at the base of the Sangre de Christos

between **7** **Chama** *(Welcome Center 505-756-2235)* and
Antonito, Colorado, a national register site traveled by the
privately operated **Cumbres & Toltec Scenic Railroad** ★
*(Chama Depot 505-756-2151. Half-day excursions also avail-
able. Mem. Day–mid-Oct.; fare)*. Coal-burning locomotives
depart from Chama's antique railyard, wind through the
San Juan Mountains and the Toltec Gorge cut by the
Los Pinos River, and chuff over the 10,015-foot Cumbres
Pass to Antonito. This is the real thing; making advance
reservations are essential.

For a look at creatures native to this country but seldom
seen, visit the **8** **Ghost Ranch Living Museum** ★ *(505-
685-4312. Tues.-Sun.; adm. fee)*, a Forest Service sanctuary
near Ghost Ranch (see sidebar page 153), to help injured
or orphaned animals unable to survive in the wild. In
1949 O'Keeffe moved to a hacienda in the village of
9 **Abiquiu** ★, renovating and refining the house—a subject of her painting—until shortly before her death in
1986 at age 98. Her airy adobe is open to the public by
advance reservation only *(505-685-4539)*. The panoramas
across the Rio Chama Valley that compelled her to relo-
cate here, however, are always at hand.

U.S. FOREST SERVICE campground reservations 800-280-2267

ARIZONA

Arizona Office of Tourism *602-542-8687* or
 800-842-8257
Road Conditions *602-255-6565*
Game and Fish Dept. *602-942-3000*
State Parks *602-542-4174*
Grand Canyon National Park *602-638-7888.*
 Campground reservations *800-365-2267*
Petrified Forest National Park *602-524-6228*
Saguaro National Park *520-733-5100*
Arizona Hotel & Motel Assoc. *602)-553-8802*
Arizona Assoc. of Bed & Breakfast Reserva-
 tion Service *602-277-0775*
Camping Information *602-650-0528*
Mi Casa, Su Casa Bed & Breakfast Reserva-
 tion Service *602-990-0682* or *800-456-0682*

NEW MEXICO

New Mexico Dept. of Tourism *505-827-0291*
 or *800-545-2040*
Road Conditions *800-432-4269*
Dept. of Game and Fish *505-827-7911* or
 800-ASK-FISH.
State Parks *505-827-7465* and *800-451-2541*
Carlsbad Caverns Natl. Park *505-785-2232*
New Mexico Bed & Breakfast statewide
 reservations *800-661-6649*

UTAH

Utah Travel Council *801-538-1030*
Road Conditions *801-965-4000*
Dept. of Fish and Game *801-538-4858*
Arches National Park *801-259-8161*
Bryce Canyon National Park *801-834-5322*
Canyonlands National Park *801-259-7164*
Capitol Reef National Park *801-425-3791*
Zion National Park *801-772-3256*

HOTEL & MOTEL CHAINS
 (Accommodations in all three states unless
 otherwise noted)

Best Western International *800-528-1234*
Choice Hotels *800-4-CHOICE*
Clairon Hotels *800-CLARION*
Comfort Inns *800-228-5150*
Days Inn *800-325-2525*
Doubletree Hotels and Guest Suites
 800-222-TREE
Econo Lodge *800-446-6900*
Embassy Suites *800-362-2779* (except N.Mex.)
Fairfield Inn by Marriott *800-228-2800*
Friendship Inns Hotel *800-453-4511*
Hampton Inn *800-HAMPTON*
Hilton Hotels *800-HILTONS*
Holiday Inns *800-HOLIDAY*
Howard Johnson *800-654-2000*

Independent Motels of America *800-841-0255*
LaQuinta Motor Inns, Inc. *800-531-5900*
LRI Loews Hotels *800-223-0888* (exc. N.Mex.)
Motel 6 *800-466-8356*
Quality Inns-Hotels-Suites *800-228-5151*
Radisson Hotels International *800-333-3333*
Ramada Inns *800-2-RAMADA*
Red Lion *800-547-8010* (except New Mexico)
Red Roof Inns *800-843-7663* (Arizona only)
Ritz Carlton *800-241-3333* (Arizona only)
Sheraton Hotels & Inns *800-325-3535*
 (except Utah)
Super 8 Motels *800-843-1991*
Travelodge International, Inc. *800-255-3050*
Westin Hotels and Resorts *800-228-3000*
 (Arizona only)
Wyndham Hotels and Resorts *800-822-4200*
 (except Utah)

ILLUSTRATIONS CREDITS

Photographs in this book are by Danny
Lehman, except for the following: Cover David
Muench; 2-3 Dewitt Jones; 10 Kathleen Revis;
27 Tom Till; 29 David Hiser; 35 David Muench;
36 David Muench; 40 Farrell Grehan; 40-41 Ric
Ergenbright; 44 Steven Mangold/WEST LIGHT;
47 Lyle Rosbotham, National Geographic Soci-
ety; 53 David Muench; 54 George F. Mobley; 55
George F. Mobley; 58 Tom Bean; 61 Jim
Richardson; 62 David Muench; 68 Larry Ulrich;
69 David Edwards Photography; 73 George H.
H. Huey; 79 Ira Block; 80 (lower) David
Muench; 82-83 Tom Bean; 85 James Randklev;
98 Willard Clay; 99 Willard Clay; 103 Larry
Ulrich; 106 Ira Block; 107 Kerrick James; 108
(lower) George H. H. Huey; 109 Clayton A.
Fogle; 113 Kerrick James; 114 Carr Clifton; 115
Jack Dykinga; 123 (lower) Michael Nichols,
National Geographic Photographer; 124 Ralph
Lee Hopkins; 126 Joel Sartore; 127 Gary R.
Zahm; 128 David Muench; 130 Richard Alexan-
der Cooke III; 131 Jake Rajs; 134 Ann Purcell;
138 Bronwyn Cooke; 149 (both) Steve
Northup; 151 David Muench; 152-153 Macduff
Everton; 154-155 Steve Northup.

NOTES ON AUTHOR AND PHOTOGRAPHER

MARK MILLER has roamed back roads for the
National Geographic Society since 1977, writ-
ing about Alaska, the Pacific Northwest, the
Rocky Mountains, and the Southwest. He is a
contributing editor of NATIONAL GEOGRAPHIC
TRAVELER and lives in Los Angeles.

NATIONAL GEOGRAPHIC has utilized photographer DANNY LEHMAN's talents throughout the
world and has published 18 of his projects.
His more than 20-year career has taken him
from the remote mountains of New Guinea to
the interior of Alaska in winter. He lives in
Santa Fe with his wife, Laurie, and two boys,
Daniel and Jonathan.

Index

157

159

160

Composition for this book by the National
Geographic Society Book Division. Printed
and bound by R.R. Donnelly & Sons, Willard,
Ohio. Color separations by Digital Color
Image, Pensauken, New Jersey. Paper by
Consolidated/Alling & Cory, WillowGrove,
Pennsylvania. Cover printed by Miken Com-
panies, Inc. Cheektowaga, New York.

Library of Congress Cataloging-in-Publication Data

Miller, Mark, 1945-
    National Geographic's driving guides to America.   Southwest, Utah,
  Arizona, and New Mexico / by Mark Miller ; photographed by Danny
  Lehman ; prepared by the Book Division, National Geographic Society.
      p.   cm.
    Includes bibliographical references and index.
    ISBN 0-7922-3425-1
    1. Southwest, New--Tours. 2. Automobile travel--Southwest,
  New-Guidebooks.   I. Lehman, Danny, 1950 June 2- II. National
  Geographic Society (U.S.). Book Division. III. Title.
  F785.3.M55 1996
  917.904'33--dc20   96-32384
                                                                        CIP

Visit the Society's Web site at http://www.nationalgeographic.com
or GO NATIONAL GEOGRAPHIC on CompuServe.